Outside the Gate

The Deception of Freedom

September 2015

Derek Rodgers

Introduction

The idea to write this book was inspired by a Bible teacher I listened to in the winter of the year 2007. The teacher stated that any problem that upsets you is a problem you are assigned to solve. The teacher also stated that any void you notice in the world is a void you must attempt to fill. The Bible teacher was informing the audience that we are not designed to be complainers and critics. We must become problem solvers. Instead of complaining about the problems in society, we must find solutions to the problems. This man I was learning from used his position to teach other men how to use their life experiences and talents to improve the world.

I developed an attitude of sharing my past experiences and knowledge with others. I possess a desire to improve the condition of my community, friends, and family. I do not see the benefit of watching those around me be destroyed. I believe that my life will become better if I help someone else become better. The people I watch destroy themselves may be the same people I need in the future. The motivation to help other young men is ignited by the memory I have of not receiving the help I needed when I was vulnerable. There were many moments when a proper word from an older man could have rescued me from heartache.

The Bible teacher helped me understand that the Creator wants men to use anything and everything they have to help others. We all have ideas, talents, gifts, wisdom, and experience that can be shared to shine light in dark places. Each one of us can assist at least one other person. Each older man can pour wisdom into a younger man. No money is needed to save someone else. One word, one idea, one smile, one laugh, one book, one sentence, one prayer, one handshake: can alter the life of a young, lost man.

The roles that we can choose to help others are infinite. A man does not need to be a licensed minister in a church to change the community. The man who promotes change does not need to be a politician. The community does not need police officers, ministers, social activists, celebrities, or popular athletes to produce change. The community needs one man to fix himself. Too much hope is placed in people with public offices. The people with the public offices are actually appointed to prevent change. (I will write about that in another book.)

A man can change the community by changing himself. A man can change the community by encouraging the young children in his neighborhood. A man can improve the life of anyone he comes into contact with by using encouraging words. His testimony and living example will provide the words and actions needed to show others how to survive and overcome situations. The role model is important to children. I learned the hard way. The young boys are always watching. The young boys remember every word you speak.

Every past experience in a man's life is a lesson that prepared him to be a problem solver. My past experiences prepared me to work with juvenile felons. My past experiences prepared me to coach youth football. I used that role to motivate the players to be more than they believe they can be. Their dreams were too small. My past has equipped me to help young men who need wisdom. Only a man can produce a man. Only a man can raise a man.

I began volunteering at Bonair in August 2008. I wanted to be a positive influence in the lives of the young men who are serving time in this juvenile prison. The role I had as a volunteer allowed me to communicate with the inmates and here their needs without the fear of ridicule or judgment. I was also watching their behavior and looking for an opportunity to help. The young men who are serving time at Bonair expressed a desire for guidance. I immediately began to remember my own experience in 1995 and 1996.

When I was in the juvenile detention center: I looked for some guidance. My friends and I wanted to believe in something or someone who could make us better. Our desire for a spiritual walk led us to become Five-Percenters. We joined the Nation of Gods and Earths. The lessons provided by the Gods and Earths provided answers and made us feel significant. We learned how to think and honor ourselves. We realized it was okay to be proud and wise. It was a different view of a Black man.

Whenever I teach a lesson at the prison, I think of what I missed when I was incarcerated. I became inspired to help these young men avoid the pitfalls that I faced in my life. A broken man will allow anyone to repair him. That is when the enemy strikes. The enemy will oppress a man when he is hungry, angry, lonely, or tired. The enemy will strike a man when he is weak physically, emotionally, and spiritually. The most common attack comes when a man does not have enough money. That is my opinion.

Job 1:6 Now there was a day when the sons of God came to present themselves before the Lord, and Satan also came among them.

Job 1:7 And the Lord said to Satan, "From where do you come?" So Satan answered the Lord and said, "From going to and fro on the earth, and from walking back and forth on it."

CHANGE

I was incarcerated on the Bonair campus in RDC in 1996. I was then sent to Barett for an 8-11 month stay. I was involved in many crimes after I was released from parole in 1997. I did not learn anything of substance about God or my true nature at Barrett. I just learned how to follow the system and play my role to get released. My heart was still hard. I learned how to act.

Acting is something that children are taught to do. It gives the appearance of obedience and submission. But any child can follow a command without giving any honor to the authority. A child will obey just to receive praise. Children have no trouble following rules. Every gang member follows rules. Every gang member can obey an order. The issue is purpose.

When I was released, I was still the same depressed and angry youngster I was when I was detained. My heart was not restored. The goal of this writing is to inform the reader about the importance of self-analysis. Change and restoration is important to obtain true freedom. This book is also for the counselor and mentor who wants to help heal a young man. The heart must be addressed. The soul needs to be redeemed.

Change and restoration are two different procedures. Change is becoming something new. Change can be positive or negative. Change is negative if it causes a bad person to act like a good person without becoming good. Change is good if it leads a bad person to alter his or hers behavior and thought. Change is limited though. Change does not alter the heart. Change can be implemented by a human or by training. Change can come from modeling another person's behavior. Change has limits. A new situation can cause the change to end.

Restoration is being returned back to the original state of perfection. Only the Creator can perform restoration. The Creator alters the heart. The Creator knows what every individual is capable of becoming. We must know the Creator. I hope this writing can lead the reader to submit to the Creator. Only the Creator can form a man into what he was originally designed to be.

Romans 12:2 And be not conformed to this world: but be ye transformed by the renewing of your mind, that ye may prove what is that good, and acceptable, and perfect, will of God.

This book was birthed by a void I observed while teaching at Bonair. I bought many books to help educate the inmates. I listened to the questions that were asked while I was teaching. I would go to bookstores searching for a book or study guide with all of the answers to all of their questions. I could never find the book that solved all of their problems. The problems that they shared and the problems I detected need to be addressed. A few of the young men reminded me of myself. History does repeat itself. These young men need to be taught. Just like I needed to be taught when I was 16 years old.

1 Samuel 12:22-24 For the Lord will not forsake His people, for His great name's sake, because it has pleased the Lord to make you His people. Moreover, as for me, far be it from me that I should sin against the Lord in ceasing to pray for you; but I will teach you the good and the right way. Only fear the Lord, and serve Him in truth with all your heart; for consider what great things He has done for you.

The only perfect book is the Bible. The problem with the inmates understanding the Bible is that most of them never read it before incarceration. The other problem is our high-tech culture. The current generation is removed from nature. The Bible is written with an agricultural mindset. The Bible contains many biological references. Most of these young men and women cannot relate to the language of the Bible. I use the Bible when I teach but I also use modern ideas, current trends and share personal experiences. Someone must take the time to teach the Bible to this generation of young men who never read.

I identified several voids in the lives of juvenile delinquents. One of the voids is a lack of knowledge. Another void is the low level of critical thinking. The new world we live in provides the idea and the image. This world removes critical thought and perverts knowledge. The constant immersion in propaganda, ads, logos, and motion pictures has reprogrammed the minds of children. This type of life has decreased actual knowledge and removed the need to learn critical thinking skills. This applies to children and adults. We are told what to think.

How many of us use our minds? Very few. We just eat, go to work, eat, come home, eat, watch TV, eat, and then go to bed. Then repeat the process the next day. We are pre-programmed.

This program is implemented in more than one way. The program produces criminals, slaves, athletes, a working class, law enforcers, prisoners, and victims. (I will write about that later. In another book.)

Many of the teenagers who attempt to live the life of crime possess weak minds and polluted hearts. Some of them get involved in crime because of their immediate environment. I believe that they can be restored to a proper, functional state with the proper leadership and wisdom. The ones who want to change need the books and the role models to teach them. The older men must teach the young men how to survive in this world. They need someone to help them change their attitudes about life and authority.

Psalm 34:11 Come, you children, listen to me; I will teach you the fear of the Lord.

I believe that 90 percent of the influences in the lives of teenagers are negative. The Bible states that the ruler of this world is the Devil. If the Bible is true, then we should not be surprised that every image on television is promoting death. It should be no surprise that the music glorifies disrespect and immoral sexual behavior. None of us should be in shock when gay people force their agenda on children. The Bible is 100% true. The children are constantly fed wicked ideas. Someone must step up and oppose the wickedness.

I believe that the people who have the ability to help the young people choose not to help them because they need help in their private lives themselves. I would admonish anyone to step up and guide the hurting; regardless of your personal condition. Do not wait until your life is perfect to help others. None of us will ever be perfect. If we wait until we are perfect to help someone else, it may be too late.

There is an advantage to helping younger men while we are experiencing struggles of our own. The trials and tribulations will allow us to show them how to handle adversity. The trials will prepare us to tell the truth. A person with no trials is not real. Adversity will produce a humble leader. We must share our tests and trials with the young ones. Show them how to walk through the valleys. There is no need to complain about the rough side of the mountain. It is the rough side of the mountain that allows us to climb to the top.

I encounter men who have the skills to assist the younger men but avoid the task because of the apparent cost. There is a risk involved in exposing oneself to broken people. But there is also a risk in not exposing yourself. The risk of not helping the brokenhearted is far greater.

I am a servant of the True and Living God. There is a price to pay for transforming lives. I will change during the process. I may change for the good. I may change for the bad. But the process of building up another man will impact me: one way or another. It is similar to the psychologists who commit suicide. They help hundreds of other people out of depression. But they end up in a state of depression themselves. We need the Lord Jesus to strengthen us in our efforts to help others.

Exodus 15:2 The Lord is my strength and song, And He has become my salvation; He is my God, and I will praise Him; My father's God, and I will exalt Him.

The cost of not helping others is a lifetime of fear. The cost of not helping others is a lifetime of isolation. The cost cannot be measured. The person you lift up may possess the gift that saves your life. The person you allow to fall may become desperate and take your life.

The teenagers who are in the streets need direction. If the older men do not help them, they will follow the street rebels. Now we have neglected children leading neglected children. The teenagers will grow with animosity towards their neighbors and become angry rebels. They will become eventually be labeled delinquents. The men who do not help them will feel separate from their realities. The men who isolate themselves from those delinquents may begin to fear them instead of love them.

These negative emotions can be eradicated by meeting together to understand each other's needs. It is possible.

The illegal life is attractive to people who do not value their existence. The illegal life is attractive to people who are not operating with a sound mind. The illegal life produces the fantasy of freedom. The fantasy destroys the real.

The older men must be willing to help expose the lies we live with and the root cause of the deviance inside of young men. Sin is real. Sin is powerful. Sin will separate a man from God.

If a man attempts to escape the presence of God, where can he go? We live our lives searching for freedom and power and never consider what the true meaning of freedom and power is. We must help each lost child consider his or hers own thoughts and actions. What is true power? What is true freedom?

What do you believe? What do you know? What do you think? What is your definition of God? What is a God? What is a man? What is the meaning of life? We all must answer these questions. We all must search for the answers to these questions. Once the answers are discovered; we live with the responsibility of the knowledge. Knowledge is power. The power to do what is right: and the power to do what is wrong.

Your answers to these questions will help expose your individual worldview. Your worldview will have a major impact on the condition of your soul.

I hope this writing is a benefit to anyone who needs to be restored to his or hers proper state. Restoration begins with the knowledge of God. Rebuilding one's life is a constant struggle to remain in communion with God. Life is incomplete without His presence.

Many elements attempt to separate us from the presence of God each day. The deception of freedom compels men to abandon God's rules in an attempt to obtain self-control. But living outside the gate God established is not freedom. We must live within God's authority to be free from our physical and mental prison. Self-will leads to Sin. Self-control leads to Sin.

Living outside the prison gate was hell for me. Many days I wanted the physical restraints to shield me from self-destruction. I never understood why in needed to be restrained until I realized I was attempting to live without God. I finally learned that I must live within his boundaries to be free of the physical prison gate.

Outside the Gate

I was incarcerated in March 1996. My second time being detained. In November 1996, I was released. I was released from Barrett Juvenile Correctional Center. I was released on parole and placed in Abraxas House. Abraxas house is a halfway house located in Staunton, VA. Abraxas House is a halfway house designed to help juvenile offenders become independent and adapt to freedom after a lengthy confinement. This was an opportunity to prove to myself and the Juvenile Justice Department that I could become a law-abiding citizen.

I still remember the fear and anxiety I felt when my counselor told me I was leaving in a few days. I was not ready for that freedom I wished to receive. I was becoming comfortable in the new system of confinement. Me and a few other inmates felt the same anxiety. We say we want to be free; but free from what? We want to be free but free to do what? It is just temporary because we have no desire to live in the other world. Who really wants to work and pay taxes every day? Who really wants to work hard to pay bills every day? The men and women living that life do not enjoy it.

No one asked me if I wanted to be released from Barrett. I knew that I was not ready for the world. No one asked me if I understood freedom. In my heart I knew that I would commit more crime. The justice system claims to be letting us free. But what some call freedom, we call it chaos. Our lives are out of order. Our families are not whole. What if an inmate does not want to go home?

No one asked me why I allowed myself to be incarcerated in 1995. The first time I was detained. No one asked me why my life was in this miserable condition.

Children are not designed for prison. How do they get there?

My depression led me to self-destructive behavior. The assumption is that I was a criminal who deserved to be confined. The assumption is that a lengthy confinement will change me. These assumptions are wrong.

The worst phase of incarceration is the sense of security and freedom that I experienced while serving my sentence. Correctional centers implement set programs and schedules. Every week of incarceration consists of set goals and pre-planned expectations. Progress is measured every week. The strict set of goals and objectives provide hope and expectation. Hope and expectation add peace to the troubled soul.

Many men do not have hope and expectation while living outside the prison system. I believe that this is the worst part of incarceration. A man should not get his goals and his hope established while in prison. His life should be planned and ordered while living with his family in the community. Prison should never substitute for the family.

The worst aspect of living free in the community again; was the lack of order and goal setting. I lived with a lot of doubt and confusion while I was free walking the streets. Living for the day was the motto. I had no idea what the future held. In a way, I was just waiting for more bad luck to send me to prison again. The media, music, and culture has a way of framing a man's mind to accept a low level of living. I did not dream of graduating college. I did not dream of having a family. I just wanted to die and start over. The key is to die with glory. Do not think that these kids dying in the streets are not welcoming the experience. Some of us want it. Death is an escape.

The lack of hope and expectation helped produce confusion and isolation. I was supposed to be happy that I was free. Instead of being happy and content, I walked with a lack of vision and no peace.

The way I viewed life while I was incarcerated contradicted the way a man is designed to perceive life. I was afraid of freedom because I did not know what to do with my ideas and energy. I endured persecution and shame whenever I exposed brilliance and independent thought. The constant opposition extinguished my fire. I allowed the enemy to remove my passion.

I felt safe in prison because I had fewer decisions to make. When I was set free, I became responsible for my own life. I will be held responsible if I ruin my life. Responsibility promotes fear in the hearts of young men. This fear is the result of seeing other men fail in their responsibilities.

Witnessing the failure of other men produces fear. If they did not succeed in life, how can I succeed in life?

This thought provoked fear in my heart. What is the way? How do I fit into a system I do not belong in? Where do I fit in? Maybe God has something for me to do; but I do not want to go to a church to find out what that destiny is.

Life is easy when a man can blame someone else for his condition. Many of us teenagers blame our situations on family, the neighborhood, or the schools. We must be taught responsibility. But who is qualified to do that? Who can teach a lost soul responsibility? The men who are wise enough to show us how to live must be available to nurture young men. I remember seeing successful men when I was young. But many of them were too concerned with their money and image to help me and my friends. This disconnect between successful people and underachieving people must be repaired.

Thousands of men return to jail and prison every year because they do not know how to live outside the gate. Maintaining freedom after being incarcerated is a challenge. How many men will admit they were afraid to be released? How many former convicts can fit into the current high-tech world? I would still like to answer a question from middle school. "Where do we fit in?" A better question is, "Are we prepared to fit in?" Some social commentators would state that we are destined to fit into the prison industrial complex. That may be true.

Men hunger for liberation and internal harmony. The problem is they do not know where to receive that liberation and harmony. A disheartened man may believe the deception that freedom is a lack of personal responsibility. The illusion that freedom is the absence of accountability is accepted by those who are mis-educated.

A prisoner has fewer responsibilities than a man who is on his own in society. A disillusioned man may enjoy the prison life. An inmate is not solely responsible for himself. An inmate has less bills, less paperwork, and less chores. The mind that has never reached its full potential may be satisfied with the life of an inmate. The mind that has been exposed to a lot of experiences and sights will be frustrated with the simple life of the penitentiary. That may explain the dumbing down of the school systems and the dumbing down of the music.

The lack of structure, critical thinking, and positive leadership in my life caused me to make thousands of bad decisions before and after I was incarcerated in 1996. It was very easy to attach myself to people who helped me destroy my life. These men and women were ruining their lives too. None of us had proper vision. None of us knew our proper function. The blind were leading the blind. The lost ones have a habit of congregating together.

Matthew 15:14 Let them alone. They are blind leaders of the blind. And if the blind leads the blind, both will fall into a ditch."

Why does a teenage boy feel more secure and free in a prison? Why does a teenage boy feel insecure and oppressed walking the streets? Why do the lost and confused people unite when none of them have the solution to their problems? Whose problem is solved when a young man destroys himself? Whose problem is being solved when young men destroy each other?

The answers to these questions will help expose the meaning of life. These questions also reveal the fact that many of our lives have no meaning. The way we live reveals that we do not understand the true meaning of life. We were lacking the proper knowledge.

We must not live outside the walls that God designed to protect us. God established boundaries to preserve our lives. The godly life must be taught at an early age. The best method of teaching would be to demonstrate the life. I wish the young men could see the life lived properly: instead of just hearing someone preach. I was never impressed with preachers when I was young. I was only impressed with men who achieved something. Most of those men were not preachers.

What this world views as oppression, God intended to be liberty. I was one of the people who attempted to find meaning by breaking God's laws. I should have remained in his hands. I should have obeyed his rules. Sin can blind you. It will blind you. I reached a certain point that did not allow me to care about spiritual matters. The rules became an obstacle I had to overcome.

The Bible is full of commandments and laws that were implemented to protect us from self-destructing. Freedom is not the absence of rules and laws. Freedom is not the absence of authority. Freedom is the absence of shame and guilt. Freedom is living under God's sovereign reign and obeying the laws of the land.

True freedom is accepting God's sovereignty in our lives. When a man is obeying God, he has less responsibilities because the Creator protects, guides, and provides for him. The True and Living God knows that we will self-destruct if we disobey Him.

The man who lives under God's rule is protected by God. The man who lives under God's authority receives security, guidance, health, and instruction from God himself. Every idea, answer, rule, and resource is in the Bible. Men were designed to live with God while abiding on the Earth. Men are free when they obey the Creator. We can experience a good living in this corrupt Earth. It is possible.

John 10:27 My sheep hear my voice, and I know them, and they follow me.

Whenever we live in rebellion to God's laws, we are outside his gate. In the book of John chapter 10; Jesus called himself the True Shepherd. When you live in rebellion to God you have chosen another shepherd. When God is not your shepherd, you lose his security and his guidance. The mistake men make is believing that living in submission to the Lord Jesus Christ leaves them powerless. The truth is that a man becomes more powerful because he is no longer operating alone.

The juvenile justice system devotes a lot of energy and research on the structure and programs utilized inside juvenile prisons. The counselors want to develop programs that teach juvenile delinquents to live efficient lives in the community. The item that deserves more attention is the teaching of the boundaries created by God. Inmates want to be outside the prison walls but fail to recognize the importance of Gods walls. If young men can focus on obeying God's rules, they can avoid being incarcerated. Living within the boundaries God established will free men from the human prison.

We want to have complete control of our own lives. We want to do the things that make us immediately happy. We want to do things that give us a sense of power. The person who chooses to rebel against God will go in the opposite direction of God's will for his life.

The opposite direction is a life of hedonism and rebellion. Hedonism and rebellion provide temporary pleasure and permanent pain. Hedonism leads to an overdose of pleasure. The overdose produces perversion because the ordinary is not good enough anymore. How many men and women have too many tattoos? How many men and women are overweight and diseased from eating too much?

The way men and women view authority must be reformed. I spent most of my life hating rules and rulers. I had very little respect for people who did not appear to benefit from following the rules themselves. I would judge people by how much wealth and power they possessed. If a person was not wealthy; I would view their rules as of no value to me. If someone who followed the rules had the attitude of a servant, I would not respect him or her. I never wanted to be a servant. I had to retain my independent thinking. (The irony is that I was never truly thinking for myself)

The only time I felt comfortable being a servant was when I submitted to a person that I believed was all powerful. I had no problem submitting to a powerful person who respected me and wanted to make me stronger. No man is willing to submit to a person who is not greater than him. Why surrender to the weak? Two weak men are just two potential victims.

I would also accept orders from a person in a higher position that I wanted to obtain. The person who gave me orders must be a person that I can admire and trust. Eventually I submitted to the supremacy of Jesus Christ. I should have done it sooner.

Jesus is God the Creator. The Creator knew that we needed goals and vision to maintain a constant path of elevation. The Creator knew that we would damage ourselves if we lost our focus.

Matthew 6:33 But seek ye first the kingdom of God, and his righteousness; and all these things shall be added unto you.

Whenever a man lacks a plan and purpose for his life, he will accept a plan and purpose from any source that promises pleasure and self-worship. A man's desire for pleasure and self-worship will lead him to sin. Sin has no limit. Sin leads to a separation from God.

Separation

Our lives lack proper direction and purpose when we are detached from our Creator. The direction of our lives is determined by God. The purpose for our lives is decided by the one who created us in the beginning. The separation of our souls from the Creator is the result of sin. Sin is the commitment to disobedient behavior. Sin is committing acts of wickedness. Wickedness is the misuse of any item, idea, or substance that you did not create. Repetitive sinful acts are the result of choosing to be separated from God. Sin is a choice produced by a prideful attitude and the need to satisfy lust.

I became separated from God because I did not want to become what I thought He desired for me to become. I became separated from God because I wanted to forge my own identity. I separated myself from God when I thought that religious people were weak and fake. Truth is that many religious people are weak and fake. But I lost my fear of God. Big mistake.

Proverbs 2:5 Then you will understand the fear of the Lord, And find the knowledge of God.

The truth is that any identity I created that opposed what God originally intended for me is wrong. The detachment from God allowed me complete control of my life. The worst thing any man can have is complete control of his own life. I read about Adam, Samson, King David, and King Solomon. If these men could not handle perfection and power; why did I think I could handle perfection and power? Even with their power; each one of those men were led astray by a woman.

How did God make us indestructible to the world; but fragile to the will of a woman?

A man in control of his own life is searching for his own purpose and meaning. That meaning may come from sources that oppose God's law. The sources that I encountered when I ignored my Creator were involved in wicked deeds. Even our positive actions were based on selfish motives. The men and women I associated with were wise in their own eyes but they had no control of their evil desires. We lived for the moment. We allowed music to change our attitudes. We let the rappers be our leaders. We would listen to anyone but God.

The people who are separated from God develop relationships and cliques to support each other. No one can survive in this world alone. We all need the clubs and fraternities because guilt and shame accompanies the man who forfeits his relationship with God. I had to surround myself with people who were not serving God to feel comfortable. We compensated for each other's lack of peace with many different distractions.

The distractions were women, parties, loud music, playing sports, and attending sporting events. Anything to ignore the voice of God. We also medicated ourselves with drugs and alcohol to feel comfort. The soul must be filled with something. Light or darkness. What is your soul filled with?

Psalm 56:13 For You have delivered my soul from death. Have You not kept my feet from falling, That I may walk before God; In the light of the living?

The Bible states that the majority of people live in rebellion to their Creator. So many people are living out of order that they do not realize they are out of order. When everyone is wrong, how do you determine what is right? In school we are taught: majority rules. But the Bible says that the majority is wrong. Imagine that.

The problem with our world is on the inside of man. The answer is outside of the man. The world thinks that the answer to our problems is on the inside. The world thinks that the problem with man is on the outside. Two opposing world views.

When I was incarcerated, we never talked about Jesus. We tried our best to avoid using the word. In 1996, we still had a fear of God. Even if we were not Christians, Muslims, or Jewish; we still had a fear of God. We loved money and pride but we did not lose all spirituality. Today, it appears that teenagers have lost their respect for God. We did not talk about Jesus because we knew how the name impacted others. We also did not know enough to prove him to be false. Islam was not intimidating because most Muslims looked like us.

Islam was the religion we talked about because it had images of Black men associated with it. Malcolm X and Louis Farrakhan made us feel like we belonged in that culture. Our souls acknowledged our need for the presence and influence of a God. But we wanted to serve God our own way. Our conceit would not allow us to admit that we needed to submit to change. The goal was to add spiritual philosophy to our own way of thinking. We masked our pride with a form of Godliness.

This method works until we need the True God. This is why it is so hard to evangelize today. Our lives are so comfortable; we do not need God. Until tragedy strikes.

God does not need man. Man does need God. Men cannot regulate the evil that exists inside them. God places a demand on the life of the man who submits to him. The separation from God gives us the ability to choose what we want in life. The natural inclination is to choose a life that contradicts the one our Creator ordained. When a man resists God, he does not remain in the same condition. He becomes dark. He must change his behavior and attitude. The change of behavior and attitude leads him to a path that he was not designed to travel. A man can only live in the light or in the darkness. No one can exist in both states at the same time.

This detachment from our Creator causes us to lead lives that allow us fit into a place we don't belong. Attempting to fit into a place that you don't belong will produce discomfort and shame. Attempting to fit into a group of men and women that you are not designed to fit into will produce insecurity and pride. You will develop a false image to maintain the improper fit. You may not be incarcerated but you are still in bondage.

The bondage is your guilt and false image. You are now living under a false identity. We are supposed to be like Jesus Christ. The God of this world is our enemy. The enemy (Devil) will allow us to adopt any image other than Jesus.

2 Corinthians 4:4 In whom the god of this world hath blinded the minds of them which believe not, lest the light of the glorious gospel of Christ, who is the image of God, should shine unto them.

I was a prisoner of a false identity for years. I behaved like other people expected me to behave: just so I can belong. This happened in religious environments and in the streets. Our families set us in certain roles. Our families do not allow us to live the way we are designed to live. I had to be fake to please other people. No one should have to be fake to belong in any group or family. Bondage is also living in a role that is not your natural position.

A man or woman must know God personally. The knowledge of self will accompany the knowledge of God. Only God can tell you who you are. This knowledge of self will prevent any man or woman from becoming fake to fit in a group. He or she will be comfortable with his or herself. When I began to know God, I never felt a need to please people again.

Men develop a lot of pride when we are involved in something wrong. Instead of removing ourselves and admitting that we are out of order, we use excessive amounts of energy to make ourselves adjust to the counterfeit role. Pride is a curse. A prideful person is cursed. A cursed person is prideful. The curse is present because of the pride. The curse remains because the pride remains. The curse is present because the person with pride does not recognize he or she is cursed. The pride will not allow a person to see that he or she is wrong.

That is why it is impossible to change a gay person. He or she is prideful. ("Gay Pride.") Pride will not allow truth to expose error. Do not waste your time. Just pray for them.

Life is stress-free when you get into the right position. Life is hard when you get into the wrong position. Sometimes pride will not allow us to remove ourselves from the life we live because we will have to admit to everyone "this is not the real me." Some men would rather die than admit to making a wrong choice. Some men would rather die than walk away from a position that he never should have had in the first place.

I lost two good jobs because of my commitment to a career in rap music. God never intended for me to make negative music. But I would not quit recording it. Pride kills the owner of it.

One of the wrong positions I attempted to fit in was becoming a drug dealer. I knew the suppliers in my city. I knew the areas that the addicts roamed. I had access to the product and the consumers. I knew all of the weed smokers. I had access to everything because of where I lived. I never looked for the business. I was living in the center of business district. The only thing I needed was a motive to enter the business.

My original dreams involved sports and music. Both of these plans were derailed by physical injuries and frustration. The lack of proper mentorship and the lack of the knowledge propelled me into the wrong direction. I am not blaming anyone else for my choices. I just know that young men need leadership when they are depressed and weak. I was lost for years. I remember a few moments when it almost looked like the people close to me were happy I was doing bad. I have heard similar stories from other men.

When I entered into darkness; every decision I made was the wrong decision. A man in darkness may not know he is making the wrong decisions. Each day is just a test of the will. Survival is the only motivation. Depression is a quiet storm. Most of us enduring depression are just waking up each day looking for a reason not to kill ourselves. Have you ever wondered why children are constantly getting high?

When everything is dark, a man does not care if he is right or wrong. The presence of God is absent from those who choose to live in sin. This is one of the reasons people hate the name of Jesus. The darkness in them becomes normal. The light provided by God reveals their error. The light provided by God also shows the flaws in a man's character.

Jesus is the light that exposes the darkness. The darkness allows the person who lives in it to ignore his or hers conscience. The darkness allows people to perform positive deeds because pride is involved in those activities. Self-aggrandizement is one of the bright lights that depressed people need to avoid suicide. But the darkness will always lead back to deviant behavior.

Positive energy will lead to the light. Love and righteousness points to God. This is why sinful men and women remain in the darkness. Pride must rule instead of love. Many of the opponents of religion understand this concept. The religious people behave with virtuous actions. But many of their deeds are motivated by pride and self-promotion. Pride is the last sin to leave a human being. Pride is the first sin to return.

My pride led me to get involved in the drug game. It was easy because of my address. One of the excuses I used to get involved in drug dealing is a common one. I was attracted by the fast money and the adrenaline rush. The drug business was also a method of developing an identity. Status is associated with the illegal life. It was instant fame.

The culture at that time made an ordinary life appear dull. I was also living with an impatience that I could not control. I found out what produced that impatience later.

The older I become; the more I realize that every man and woman needs a partner. Jesus sent his disciples on their missions in sets of two. We need a brother or sister to walk with in this life. This is especially true for teenagers. The choices we make as teenagers affect our lives forever. I can recall many moments in my life where I just needed one word from an elder or mentor. That one word would have prevented years of heartache.

Psalm 90:12 So teach us to number our days, that we may apply our hearts unto wisdom.

Drug dealing was a choice that was available because of my neighborhood. I was not born to be a hustler but the climate of the culture permitted my participation. The True and Living God does not produce drug dealers. The Creator never intended for me to get involved that life. I did not look for weed and crack. It was in front of my house.

The separation from God is the beginning of many other issues that lead to my eventual self-destruction. I got involved with different religions, illegal activities, and thieves. I studied many different philosophies to find excuses for my condition. I wanted to find a way to live without Christianity. I did not want to be like the others who followed Christianity. Their lives were a mess. I had to find another way. I was eagerly hoping for a better way. This desperation was enhanced by the fact that when I did attempt to live that life; my situation only became worse.

I had this hunger inside me to rescue and help other people, but I could never find the proper help for myself. This also proved to be a lesson I was required to learn. A drowning man cannot rescue another drowning man. One will sink the other one to breathe. Two drowning men need a third person who is not drowning to save them both.

The shame and the guilt that accompanied my rebellion led me to use and abuse alcohol and other drugs. I also abused my body by sleeping with many different women. Unsafe and reckless behavior was the high I needed to get through each day. I was neurotic. Refusing to fit in when I could. Many men in my condition join the Army. The commercial asks, "Do you want to be somebody?" Many of us are lost souls.

Men become abusers of themselves because we are at odds with God. God does not have to kill us. We will eventually destroy ourselves. A man cannot destroy God so he destroys everything that reminds him of God's glory. This attitude aided in my deep depression and eventual incarceration. I firmly believe prison has saved many lives. Prison delays the self-destruction. In many cases, prison prevents self-destruction.

Slave Mentality

A slave is a person who does not have the ability to think for his or herself. A slave is a person who lacks the freedom to choose his or hers actions. A slave is also a person who does not know what to do. He or she is ignorant. I would also say a slave is a person who is so uninformed that he or she does not know that he or she is a slave.

Harriet Tubman once stated that she could have freed twice as many slaves if they only knew that they were slaves. A man or woman must know that he or she is in bondage to an idea, substance, or a system to be set free from the idea, substance or system.

I was a slave for years. I did not have the freedom or the courage to think for myself. I did not have the opportunity to think for myself in certain situations. Some of the people that ruled over me did not teach me how to develop critical thinking skills. Some of my leaders did not have the ability to think outside the box.

It may appear that people are forced into servitude and feeble thinking. The pattern I see is one of fear. I chose to be a follower at several points in my life. I was afraid of my own power. I was afraid of the opposition that constantly arose when I walked in my true calling. Men are shown images of Malcolm X, JFK, and Martin Luther King, and Jesus being assassinated for doing something good for their people. These images subconsciously make men fearful.

Genesis 46:3 And he said, I am God, the God of thy father: fear not to go down into Egypt; for I will there make of thee a great nation:

A weak leader may want weak followers. Who is your leader? I encountered people with high positions who do not want men to be able to think for themselves. I encountered these people in churches, schools, and in the streets. This power struggle affected me in a negative way. Sometimes I thought that my free thinking was a curse. Sometimes, I would act dumb to avoid conflict.

How many times have you kept your mouth shut when you knew in your spirit; you should have spoken up? Your destiny is waiting for your courage.

I was in a state of depression and dominated by pride. My pride would prevent me from being truthful with myself. Pride itself may be the devil. At times I did not realize I was living beneath my ability. I would refuse to believe that I could do better.

I remember the day my brother drove to Virginia and spent the night in my house. He asked me why there were no lights in the house. I did not realize how dark it was in my own home. I liked it dark. I probably had a hundred excuses for it too.

What darkness have you grown accustomed to? What evil has become acceptable in your life?

Every gift God gave humans may also be a curse. We have this amazing ability to adapt to harsh circumstances. The curse of this ability is how easily we can adapt to situations that we should be changing. I became comfortable in the dark.

Without a true light, no man can recognize that he is lost. Many men and women suffer from the same conditioned experience. No true light.

Psalm 56:13 For You have delivered my soul from death. Have You not kept my feet from falling, That I may walk before God, In the light of the living?

The Creator intended for men to be kings. Men are designed to lead their wives and children. Men are designed to lead their communities. We are kings on Earth as long as we obey him as children.

The Creator intended for each man to be responsible for himself. Men are expected to be free thinkers and leaders of their homes and families. Each man must be equipped. Each man must know how to think, live, and behave like a leader. I was not prepared to become that king or leader. My mind was weak and my behavior was immature. I never had the equipment. If I had it, I did not know how to use it.

Why are so many men who want to do good constantly losing? Some say it is by choice. Some say it is the devil. Some say it is the White man oppressing the Black man. (Then why are so many White men ungodly? Why are millions of White men in prison, too? The issue is bigger than race.) The answer is in the Bible. Jesus said this world will hate you for being good.

John 17:14 I have given them Your word; and the world has hated them because they are not of the world, just as I am not of the world.

No man can become a king with a slave mentality. I heard this phrase while attending a Hebrew Bible study class in 2011. The teacher of the class informed the students we must have the proper ingredients to improve our lives. The teacher impressed on us the importance of education, humility, patience, and love. Every man must be taught to live and think like a CEO before he can be promoted to a CEO position. A man must be prepared to play professional basketball before he is drafted and hired to play professional basketball. The key in life is realizing that a person must be prepared in advance to receive a promotion. No one is promoted to a leadership position before he or she can handle the responsibilities of a leadership role. As long as a man exhibits poor thinking skills, he will never be expected to function as a leader. The work must be done in advance. No man can become a leader with a slave mentality.

This concept is very important to a man's development. I have a habit of attempting to skip several steps in training. I have a history of selecting shortcuts in projects and chores. I hate waiting for an expected result. If I can see the final outcome, I will begin to lose interest in the many steps necessary to complete the task. I will want to fast forward to the end. Shortcuts destroy the purpose of the training. Character is developed while enduring the process of improvement. Shortcuts hamper the development of character.

I would suggest, in order to become a king, a man must be trained and nurtured by kings. A woman cannot do it. The streets cannot do it. Luck cannot do it. Only a person who has achieved a higher level can raise another person up to that level. A mother can prepare a son to be raised up. But a mother cannot make him something she is not. A father who has not reached his full potential can equip his son to be raised up; if he is not capable of doing it himself. The father must grow in order for his son to grow.

Shortcuts, cheating, and lying cannot make a boy become a whole man. No man who made it to the top in an unethical manner remained on top without continuing his unethical behavior. That man had to continue lying, cheating, and stealing to maintain that position. Every decision has a consequence.

A young man must be mentored by mature men who will teach him the proper way to think and behave. If a young man returns to his old companions, he will not change. I personally benefited from older mentors. It is easier to help someone if you already graduated from his current experience.

A mentor should be at least a decade older than the student. If a mentor is the same age as his mentee, he may not be entirely honest. His pride may prevent him from sharing his own faults. I had bad experiences learning from men close to my age range. We were good partners and associates but it was not wise to consider them teachers. They had faults of their own. They had issues that they hid from me. Eventually, they became liars or just fake. It was also irresponsible of me to place that burden on them. There are times that we should not hand people burdens that they cannot bear.

A mentor who is older than his pupil will be transparent and absolutely honest. The experienced, older elder will not be ashamed to reveal his past errors and share knowledge. The elder mentor is not concerned with his power and protecting a reputation. The mature and older mentor will be fortified with integrity because he already overcame his character deficits.

The world needs more godly mentors. Public schools need more godly mentors. Churches need more godly mentors. What if more people were just godly? Each man and woman would be inspirational by default.

Proverbs 13:20 He that walks with wise men shall be wise: but a companion of fools shall be destroyed.

The Bible commands the older men to teach the young men. My generation suffered from a lack of proper leadership. We listened to the wrong men for advice and information. Our lecturers and tutors were hip-hop artists and disillusioned adults who were filled with envy, bitterness, and regret. I was surrounded by men who hated anyone with more money and a higher level of education. Unfortunately, these older men remained slaves while programming younger men into becoming slaves. We need Godly teachers.

Young, impressionable people should avoid those older men and women who missed their destiny. The people who missed their opportunities will molest the minds of the young who have dreams and goals. They will infest the minds of the young with fear, doubt, prejudice, and anxiety. The people who accomplished nothing with their lives will prevent others from achieving their dreams. They do it through speech and brainwashing. I have seen this happen. I call those people "dream snatchers."

Speech is very powerful. Be careful how you use your words. Children do not forget what you say to them. I only speak positive words to my children. They will always overcome their obstacles. They see a positive future. They also know that they will be guided by God.

Psalm 34:13 Keep your tongue from evil, And your lips from speaking deceit.

A man who behaves like a slave will be compelled to forfeit his slave mentality. The man who wants to mature must let go of his negative thinking. Eradicating the mind of negative thinking will require the eliminating of negative people. This becomes an issue when those negative people are family members. The truth is that many of the negative people in our lives are close friends and relatives. It is very easy to waste your life by remaining on a low level of existence because your friends and relatives are underachieving. The problem comes when you attempt to rise. And those people hold you back.

The slave must forget his past teachings and separate himself from his previous environment. My life did not become better until I separated from my hometown and severed all connections to my old friends. The new city I moved to was Stone Mountain, GA. The change of residence allowed me to think free. I felt like I could start over. I did not know what to expect. I just felt like God was pushing me. The only thing I knew was that I did not want to spend the rest of my life in prison. Peer pressure does not exist when you don't have a reputation to protect. I had a chance to start over in 1998.

Georgia

The move to Georgia gave me a chance to do what I wanted to do without trying to please other people. (Ironically, I did not know what I wanted to do.) The move to Georgia was not planned, but the change of residence was performed at a critical moment. The situations that continued to replay in my life were destructive. The situations were the result of bad choices I made in high school. The situations were negative because the people I associated with were corrupt. My past decisions attracted people that should not have been in my life at all. I had to leave Newport News.

I developed negative friendships when I was in a state of delusion and depression. I surrounded myself with people while I was depressed: that I would not have surrounded myself with if I was not depressed. Sick people attract sick people. Wealthy people attract wealthy people.

Wise people attract wise people. Healthy people attract healthy people.

Isaiah 24:22 And they shall be gathered together, as prisoners are gathered in the pit, and shall be shut up in the prison, and after many days shall they be visited.

When I was released from Barrett in 1997, I wanted to change the direction of my life. But I went back to the same neighborhood. I was also surrounded by the same people. I had enough common sense to know I did not want to spend the rest of my life in prison. Changing my direction meant changing everything. The change was almost impossible while living in the same city. I could not do it on my own. I still had trouble understanding the real me.

I had an easier time changing my behavior and attitude in Georgia. I was in a new city with new people. I did not have to worry about what my old friends thought about me and my new attitude. Fear was not a motivating factor in my life. My motivation was to learn a new way to live. I was hoping that there was more to life than working 9-5 and being broke. There had to be another way.

Some of my old dreams were resurrected while living in Georgia. My old ideas were coming back to my memory. Opportunities that I thought were impossible became possible while living in Georgia. I was now an entrepreneur and an artist. I could surround myself with other entrepreneurs and other artists. You will always surround yourself with people who possess the same spirit. We attract the type of person we are. You will always attract the type of person you are.

Amos 3:3 Can two walk together, except they be agreed?

The term used to describe transformation in the Bible is 'born again'. An immoral man must be born again to become a good man. Being born again is a transformation process. I was being transformed while living in Georgia. The process was painful to endure.

The transformation was not a dramatic transformation. The renovation of my soul was a long, slow process. I did not view my life as something extraordinary. I was immersed in the day-to-day duties of working and avoiding conflict. I began to view every day as a gift. I did not want to become an adult in the adult prison system. I did not realize the purpose of this season of my life. I did not know I was beginning a restoration process. The True and Living God was involved when I did not know he was involved.

The transformation in my life became evident every time I traveled back to Virginia. While I was in Georgia, I was busy learning how to become responsible for myself. I was learning how to deal with the rat race called the American way. I was learning how to avoid conflict and resist temptation.

The rat race is not friendly to anyone. Our American culture is complicated. It is better than any other country I know of. But it is hard to motivate oneself to get up and work. Every day. The other challenge is defining a specific purpose. My challenge was adjusting to the high-tech world. Where do I fit in? The subculture of hip-hop can leave a man immature. The subculture of hip-hop can leave a man in a state of rebellion. The hunger to succeed in America is the result of wanting a reward for the pain endured every day. I wanted to be wealthy overnight because of the pain I endured in the past. But that is not how the system operates.

I did not realize how much I matured and undergone a change of heart. The change was recognized when I was back in my former environment. I was not impressed with the way my old friends were living. I did not have a desire to participate in the same acts that were attractive in the past. Smoking weed was not amusing anymore. I started to understand that getting drunk every day was a waste of time.

In high school, I had no goals or responsibilities. I was depressed and bored. Getting high and drunk did not cost me anything in high school. When I could not play football; I didn't care if I graduated. Times change. The mind changes. It is supposed to change.

In high school, the attitudes we lived with appeared acceptable. The rebellious life we called street life was supposed to be the standard of living. Everyone could not submit to the rules. Every child is not built the same.

A good example is my friend who would not play high school basketball. I can't use his name. But he was the best player in the Denbigh area. He would not play ball in high school because of the rules and expectations. It is crazy how life plays out. If he did play, he would have been a division I scholarship athlete. He could not handle high school. His mother had personal issues. I know the whole story. How do we treat the ones who are not equipped to submit to society's rules? Life is not fair. Fair is a myth.

Many of us were afraid of the real world. Most of us were not equipped to survive in the real world. The real world only benefits those who work hard. The real world benefits those who control those workers. It is a hard life. It is a monotonous life. It is also an unfair life. I dealt with a lot devilish people in the legal, blue collar world. The law abiding citizens were no better than the street criminals I knew.

Truth is the real world benefits those who know how to cheat and not get caught. Bill Clinton proved that concept to be true. The false preachers on television prove that life is not fair. The wealthy people who commit crime and never serve prison time are evidence that life is not fair. How do we nurture children into a world that is corrupt? Only the Bible has the answer.

I had some success working for various companies. I opened a bank account and paid a few bills. But that life was not satisfying. I wanted something more. Many of my friends felt the same way.

I was treated unjustly on several jobs. I was lied on by coworkers on several different occasions. It is a challenge to maintain composure after enduring injustice. I was constantly tempted to commit new crimes to make money. A few days I did. Atlanta is a very large city. I was able to do my dirt and escape.

I noticed the vanity of the street life as I became more mature. It is the ultimate high. It is very exciting. I felt above the law for a while. But in the end; that life is not profitable. That mindset is designed to produce self-destructive men. Self-destructive men resist education and self-improvement. The mindset that is fortified from that lifestyle is one that avoids God.

One of my friends would always say that he would never attend college. He was a very proud man who thought he had all the answers. It is amazing how our pride can prevent us from becoming better people. College is a good avenue to understanding how to function in America. There is a reason foreigners come to America and enroll in college. There is a reason foreigners come to America and make a priority to send their children to college.

When I visited my old neighborhood; I began to realize how poor I was thinking in the past. When I was in the dark, I attracted dark people. When I began searching for the light, I attracted people who were walking in the light. I see my old neighborhood as a learning center. I learned a million lessons in Courthouse Green.

The irony of my transformation is that it altered my view of my past in Newport News. I was still committing crime in Georgia. I was still drinking almost every day in Georgia. My mindset was different; but I found a way to commit to the same behaviors. My soul was changing but I could not alter my actions. I did not have the Holy Spirit yet.

The alcohol was cheap and sold on almost every street corner. I was visiting dozens of nightclubs and bars on the weekend. Instead of sitting on the curb drinking all night long; I was in the club drinking. Instead of standing on the corner smoking weed all day; we were in the parking lot outside of Club 112 smoking. Same behaviors in a new setting. It looks different but it is not different.

Leviticus 26:19 And I will break the pride of your power; and I will make your heaven as iron, and your earth as brass:

God wanted me to change my behavior but I wanted to be free from his presence. I wanted to believe that I could change myself all by myself. Pride prevented me from allowing God to do his finished work.

The worst thing God can do is let a man control his own life. It will always lead to misfortune. I was incarcerated twice while living in Georgia. I was issued a dozen traffic tickets in Georgia. I was still reckless with my actions. The reasons were discovered later. But the damage is already done.

I started two small businesses. They both failed. I learned a lot about myself and the culture. I learned that manipulation is needed in the business field. The same hustles used in selling drugs and prostitution must be used in the legal business institutions. It is the same game. The only difference is that one is legal and the other is illegal.

The problem with attempting to be at one with God and changing from a life of rebellion; is the fact that living a legal life may still fiend off the negative characteristics of a man. I was still lying, scheming, and manipulating people to sell my products. I was still lusting for power and recognition. I was still attempting to become an idol. I was still attempting to be someone I was not. I was still the same person. The only difference was my address and my vocation.

Maybe my business ideas failed because God knew I would just become a stronger version of my former prideful self. Maybe God allowed me to fail. I don't know, maybe.

Job 31:3 Is it not destruction for the wicked, And disaster for the workers of iniquity?

Restoration takes time because the consequences must be endured. Life is not like the ending of Hollywood movies. Our problems are not solved in two hours. I wish they were.

Value

Value is something I learned while living on my own. I learned what to value and what not to value. I also recognized that I did not value anything. I hardly valued my life. I viewed my life as a series of failures. I allowed the world to make me feel insecure and worthless. A lot of men feel this way. That is one reason men leave their wife and children. The world breaks us.

The subject of value became obvious when I visited my home town. I recognized how easy it was for my people to risk their lives. I would see them continue to sell drugs and risk their lives for small amounts of money. We place very little value on our lives. This troubled me because I was not willing to take those same risks. I had a son. I did care about his life. He made me want to live. I wonder what would have happened if he was not born.

I began to value my life when I realized that there was more to life than living for the streets. The world looked different when my address changed. I wanted to act right but I did not have the power to act right. It is sad to admit I cannot control myself.

Romans 7:21 I find then a law, that, when I would do good, evil is present with me.

My first son was born in the year 2000. He was born in Georgia Baptist Hospital in Atlanta, Ga. His birth was another reason I placed more value on my life. His birth was one of the most dramatic events in my life. I never thought I would see the birth of my own child. I dreamed of having a son but never thought it would happen. So many of my other dreams never manifested. This one became real. I was a broken, angry man who is now a father. Now I need to learn the true definition of value. I could no longer be selfish.

Psalm 53:2 God looked down from heaven upon the children of men, to see if there were any that did understand, that did seek God.

The birth of my son compelled me to view the future with his needs in mind. I had to prepare his future and find a reason for him to live. I needed a reason for him to live because the world seemed to be unfair to me. I knew that the world would treat my son the same.

This new pattern of thinking forced me to judge myself every day. I would ask myself, "What have I done to make my child's life better?" I would ask myself, "What have you done to make your life better today?"

I never knew how to control and manage my thoughts, feelings, and emotions at the same time. My value system was affecting my thoughts, feelings, and emotions. When I was expected to be happy I was sad. When I was expected to be sad I was happy. Our lives have been so inconsistent. Many of us do not function the way we should. This twisted thinking is seen when inmates lengthen their sentences when it is time to go home. Instead of feeling joy when it is time to be released on parole: the inmates feels fear and panic. He chooses to commit an institutional offense and stays.

The lost soul enjoys pain. Similar to the card player who stays at the table until he loses. I was afraid of people who were good. I felt comfortable with people who were unhappy. What is wrong with us? Why do we enjoy pain so much? Why do we generate situations that cause us to lose?

I felt uncomfortable with people who were always happy. Their kindness would force me to trust them. Trust made me vulnerable. I did not want to be vulnerable. Some people wake up happy. Some people wake up unhappy.

A man must identify his own value system. His value system will identify his agenda and his motives. A man's value system will determine his friends and associates. A man who values sports will surround himself with athletes. A man who values knowledge will surround himself with scholars. A man who values the street life will surround himself with criminals and thieves. What do you value?

What instigates you to keep living? What will you never compromise?

I had to ask myself where my values came from when I started to change my life. What desire was on the inside of me? Why did I want to do better? I remember when I worked at the Macy's furniture factory in Tucker, Ga. One day a coworker asked me what motivated and inspired me. I did not have a real answer. I just freestyled something to make myself appear deep. I spent the rest of the day asking myself the same question.

What was it that inspired me to write my songs? What was it that inspired me to maintain my integrity at work? What made me different than my coworkers who were sniffing coke and smoking weed at the job? That is what my associate wanted to know. What makes you different?

The source of a man's values will reveal his major influence. The major influence in a man's life will decide if he remains in the light or it may transport him to the dark side. What is the influence? Is the influence media, people, or objects? Every influence can be placed in three categories.

Power, money, or sex. These three categories can define every choice a man makes. These three categories will identify a man's values. The Bible uses three other labels. The Bible calls the three major factors of decision making as: lust of the eyes, lust of the flesh, and the pride of life. Very similar. We can split hairs about how we lust and chase our fantasies. It is not a priority to choose labels. What we must do is identify how and why we think the way we do.

Exodus 20:17 *"You shall not covet your neighbor's house; you shall not covet your neighbor's wife, nor his male servant, nor his female servant, nor his ox, nor his donkey, nor anything that is your neighbor's."*

The common values maintain a society are health, family, respect, and peace of mind. These concepts are necessary to allow communities to thrive. Each man and woman must coexist on the same land. If everyone abandoned order and followed their own fantasies: cities and towns would collapse into anarchy.

The Ten Commandments admonish men and women to honor their neighbors. Treat others the way you want them to treat you. One must respect the neighbor's life, property, and family. It is the only way we can live together.

The dark side changes all of these values. When I was walking in darkness; I only valued power, submissive women, and self-rule. Men are constantly warned not to live for themselves. I had many opportunities to change my life but I could never find the strength. I had too much fun living for my own selfish desires. I continued to ignore the inner prompting from my Creator.

Matthew 5:8 Blessed are the pure in heart: for they shall see God.

I had some internal conflicts that I was not aware of. I wish that every man could find time to meditate and pray. I wish that our culture had more moments of silence. I was consumed with fixing my obvious problems that were visible. I did not heal some of my subconscious issues. We need time to examine our own minds and remove all toxic ideas. One wrong idea caused mass destruction in my life. One lie produced a million other problems. Identify the root of your malfunction. If you can find it.

Examine your values. Where did they come from? How do they affect your thinking?

The Lies we Live With

The birth of my son was eight months after the most revealing moment of my life. My 21st birthday was the scariest event of my adult life. Every time I was arrested I was not scared. I was not afraid to be incarcerated. I knew what to expect in jail. I knew how to handle a police officer. I feel fear when an enemy was shooting at me. Bullets are hot. I engaged in fifty to sixty street fights. Those situations are manageable. Pain is temporary. Those moments are deserved and expected. I asked for that. But how does a man wrestle with his imagination and become victorious? How does a man face his subconscious mind and not lose control of his mind?

The night before my 21st birthday I was full of panic. I was afraid to go to sleep and I did not know why. I tried to hide my fear the best way I knew how. I stayed busy and I maintained my sense of humor throughout the day. When midnight approached; I was afraid to go to sleep. I spent most of the evening in the apartment with my future wife. I was afraid to leave the apartment and I did not know why. Where did this fear come from?

We live with so many lies. We live with many different lies and do not realize how much these lies damage our thinking. These lies will take root if they are not removed immediately. Each one of us must identify these lies and eradicate them. Then tell someone else it is a lie.

These invisible ideas that torment our minds are sometimes labeled demons. Some spiritual people label them evil spirits. That may be debatable but their impact is not up for debate. The power of a lie is enormous. These ideas are especially powerful when you do not know they exist. The thought is invisible; but the influence of the lie manifests in our actions.

At midnight I had a nervous breakdown. I began to weep uncontrollably. I had no obvious reason to cry and I was not feeling any physical pain. The moment was so overwhelming that I lost control. My future wife did not know what to do because I had never behaved like this before. She just knelt beside me and put her arms around me. I still had no explanation. The lies we live with.

I think I wept for 30 minutes. The moment felt like time froze. I just remember being stuck on the floor hearing some voices that did not come from my girlfriend. My brother was in the apartment but he was in another room. I was just frozen. When I did begin to manage my thoughts, I started to realize that this moment resembled the frozen moments I had as a child.

These moments were the occasions when I felt the whole presence of God. As a child I did not really know God; I just knew that there was an entity bigger than me. I remember singing the name of Jesus. But I did not know him the way I should have known him. That shallow relationship was enough as a child. I did know God was real. I just avoided religions. Only God can tell me what to do.

This time I believe he was attempting to relay a message. I decided to humble myself and listen. It was easy to enter a state of humility after crying in front of my lady for 30 minutes. God obviously knew who I was and wanted to make contact. Whatever God had to say must be important. I was broken and did not know why. The lie I was living with needed to be eradicated.

The message I received from the Creator that night was something that I did not understand until He allowed me to recall some subconscious thoughts that were stored in my mind. The reason I was in a state of fear the night before my

21st birthday is because I thought I would die before my 21st birthday. I internalized a lie that was being taught in Black churches when I was a teenager. The elders and some of the ministers would tell us that Black men lived with two strikes against them. The two strikes would cause my one mistake to lead to my death before I reached the age of 21. I believed this lie.

I allowed that statement to dominate my mind. I heard this statement from several different sources throughout my life. This lie was presented in religious settings and in the media. I heard this lie in the streets. I believed it because I heard it in church and in the community. At some point during my high school years, I accepted the lie that I would die before my 21st birthday. What lie are you living with?

What lie are you living with? What lie is preventing you from fulfilling your life's purpose? What lie is causing you to destroy yourself? What lie freezes your potential?

What lie is ruining your family? What lie will not let you grow? What lie will not let you go?

Job 27:4 My lips will speak no evil, and my tongue will speak no lies.

The Bible states that life and death is in the power of the tongue. Many different religions and cultures teach people that words have power. This one statement altered my whole existence. I honestly did not know how much of an impact that one idea affected my life. When I had this nervous breakdown, I believe I heard God telling me that he knew I did not expect to live that long. I also believe that he was telling me that he wanted to control the rest of my life. I also believe that he reminded me that he promised to preserve my life.

I don't want to put words in God's mouth but I must attempt to explain the moment. God makes us promises all the time. The promises are written in the Bible text. We just don't believe it is God talking. What the saints hear is written in the Hebrew Scriptures.

Joshua 23:10 One man of you shall chase a thousand, for the Lord your God is He who fights for you, as He promised you.

We must learn how to recognize the difference between God's voice, our own mind, and our memories. The positive and negative memories play a major role in our decision making now. Studying the Word of God will purify the mind.

God told me that he would protect me when I was a child. I chose to believe that when I was young. When I became a teenager, religious people told me that Black men are expected to die before they are 21. That human belief system contradicted what the Creator said. It is usually people who claim to know God who war against God.

The false religious leaders are the people who teach children wrong ideas about God. These people are poisonous. These people poison and corrupt those they come into contact with. I was poisoned. My weak and pliable mind accepted a lie. One of the negative aspects of religion is how a child will accept a fable because of blind devotion.

The lies we live with create an irrational philosophy. The lies we live with affect every decision we make. I made a lot of decisions based on the idea that I would not live long. I began living for the moment when I was in high school. The fear of dying before I was 21 created an impatience inside me that caused maniac behavior. I did not even know I was impatient and full of fear. I thought the courage I displayed was fueled by strength. The courage I displayed was driven by fear. That fear produced a great depression.

Isaiah 26:3 You will keep him in perfect peace, Whose mind is stayed on You, Because he trusts in You.

The lies we live with are so deep that we must acknowledge them as soon as possible. I made thousands of bad decisions because I did not know I would be alive this long. I refused to commit to people and ideas because of my fantasy of an early exit. I remember having an opportunity to enroll in college in 1997. I chose not to go because it was an apparent waste of time. I could not see 10 years ahead.

Imagine how many young men lost their lives because of this lie. How many men died early because they did not expect to see adulthood? How many other lies are ruining the lives of men? And young women?

How many young men lived the street life because they could not see themselves at 30 or 40 years old? Now they are 30 or 40 years old in prison. What lies are you living with? What lie paralyzes you whenever an opportunity comes?

The ideas and concepts of life we accept as children play a role in our adult decision making. Every choice you make is based on how you view the world and your position in the world. Do you believe that you do not deserve better? Do you believe that living good is wrong? Are you a permanent servant or slave? How do you view life?

A friend of mine uses the phrase "belief-window'. What is it that you believe? What is the meaning of life in your belief-window? What is your reason for living?

I did not plan on living a long life. The idea that I would not live past 21 years of age prevented me from going to college. I viewed college as a waste of time. Why waste four years of my life if the education will not benefit me. I would have graduated at the age of 22. I did not have enough patience to start a legal business because I thought it would not be fully functional until I was in my 30's. Most of the legal lifestyles take years to develop and maintain. I did not want to waste the time I had left. (The time that I thought I had left.)

I also became risky in my pursuit of amusement and pleasure. I was a drug abuser and an alcoholic. Why be healthy if I am going to die early? I never used protection when I was sleeping with different women. I overdosed on pleasure. An overdose of pleasure only leads to deep depression. I did not value my future. I failed to prepare for the future. There are many different ways to play Russian roulette with your life.

My friends and I used to drive high and drunk every day. My friends and I would chase and conquer every woman that gave us a chance. We would also look for parties to attend every night. Instead of looking for enterprises to start, we desired instant gratification. This behavior was instigated by the fact that I thought I would not be living long. This risky behavior was a symptom of not believing I had a future.

A child without a future is a dangerous person. A child without a future will gamble his life tonight; because he sees no tomorrow. He or she will risk it all. That is a dangerous person. A person with nothing to live for. A child without a future is a danger to his family, friends, and community. Some people call the child with no cares America's nightmare.

America's Nightmare

A child without a future is a dangerous person. A child without a future can be used as a weapon. A child with no hope for the future has the potential of becoming a weapon of mass destruction. This phenomenon is evident in the school shootings. A fearless child is a bomb waiting to explode. These children will spread destruction and violence wherever they go.

Children listen to social commentators who supply their motivation to remain violent and destructive. Hip-hop artists and musicians present death and destruction in their work to incite mass destruction. Millions of dollars are earned by supporting violence and drug abuse. An industry that thrives off the pain of the people must produce people to supply the pain.

The mass destruction is implemented on several different planes. The planes are the mind, the body, and the social structure. One idea can destroy a child's mind. The child will then destroy his or hers own body. The ruined children will now cause social disorder. Destruction and growth operate in cycles. The cycle must be completed. The goal is to begin the proper cycle. Only good ideas can be shared. Only positive words should be spoken to children.

The disorder begins within the family. The dysfunctional family becomes a curse to the community. One corrupt family torments an entire community. History proves that a minority of uncivilized people have the potential to destroy the entire nation that they inhabit. Parents must take the time to be purified and restored. This is essential for the parents to raise and nurture whole children.

The people who want to preserve a nation must have hope for the future. The people who have no hope for the future destroy their nation by only living for the moment. The people with hope live for the future and enjoy each moment. Hopeless children live with high risk decisions.

The hopeful people live with constructive and conservative decisions.

Secular music serves the agenda of the company that employs the artists. Most of the entertainment on the radio is not about preservation. The music is about hedonism and rebellion. Record companies seek out an audience of lustful people. The uncontrolled lust leads to anarchy, rebellion, violence, and various forms of lawlessness.

One hip-hop artist has the power to destroy the minds of a million people with one song. One soul singer can write lyrics that produce hedonistic behavior in millions of teenagers. One dangerous man can function as a weapon of mass destruction. History proves that one song can alter human thought. History proves that one man can introduce an idea that builds or destroys a nation. The devil only needs one person.

The hip-hop and rock and roll artists who do not value their own minds or life will pass their negative attitudes on to the audience who listens to them. The spirit of the one who writes the lyrics will pass on to the listener. I remember feeling like I knew the musician after I listened to his or hers music. A person's mind is transferred through their art.

Four of my friends are in prison now for robbing and killing a police officer. These men would sit in their apartment all day and night listening to rap music. I still remember the names of the CD's and tapes that they played. I remember the lyrics of those songs. I can remember their attitudes changing. Two of them became dropouts before the murder. The ingredients were present for self-destruction.

I remember the spirit of that apartment. We would just sit there and think of the evil acts we could commit. Our minds were never attached to anything productive. We just wanted to wild out. We were dancing with the devil. The music and the weed sent us into another state of consciousness. Anyone who says that music does not carry a spirit is not telling the truth.

This is just an example of what happened to thousands of us. We begin to immerse ourselves in negative environments. We surround ourselves with negative people. We listen to negative commentators. Only negative behaviors will be produced from this combination.

It is not fair to put all the responsibility on the music. But who can deny the impact that one idea has on a teenage brain? Who can deny that music influences thought? Who can honestly state that music does not transport a spirit? My friends and I are still responsible for our actions. The lyrics in music helped compel us to perform the negative actions we probably already wanted to perform.

The ideas we receive through music must be rejected. Or those ideas will be accepted. Only God can remove the ideas after they have been implanted. The mind must be reprogrammed. Every man I grew up with was not polluted.

I still wonder how some of my friends avoided the pitfalls I fell into.

The term America's nightmare is used in songs and movies. The term describes a person who is violent, callous, and rebellious. The term was also used to describe young, Black, men who refuse to obey the law and respect authority.

The social commentators who presented this image of young men (Black, White, and Spanish) are the same commentators who earned money through the publication of this image. The theme, America's Nightmare, makes money for Hollywood, record companies, and clothing stores. The stockholders who invest in private prisons profit from the use of this image. Young men who have no hope for the future are stored in the private prisons. America's nightmare has become a profitable instrument.

The young men who are labeled America's nightmare or a menace to society must also realize that being a criminal adds value to their lives. Inmates are worth money to prison owners. Inmates in prisons and penitentiaries are cheap labor. Criminals in the street increase profits for security corporations and manufacturers of security equipment. The sale of drugs and alcohol are dependent upon criminals and drug abusers. Every life is valuable. Your life will benefit God and your family, or your life will benefit the criminal justice system. Your actions will also benefit ATF. ATF is the Bureau of Alcohol, Tobacco, and Firearms. The government earns money from the commission of crime. A child may not believe that he or she has a positive future, but that child's life is valuable to somebody.

Every man, woman, or child has value. That value is determined by your behavior. Someone is profiting from every decision you make. You can get a legal job and be a contributor to the country by paying taxes. The alternative is living an illegal life and becoming an inmate who makes a profit for the private corrections industry. You will work somewhere as long as you live. The variable is how long do you plan to live? The first question is, "do you want to live?" If you do want to live, "Why?"

The infamy that accompanies the role of America's nightmare may appear attractive. The sense of power produced by infamy compensates for the loss of pure identity. You will enjoy the fear and respect people have for you. My reputation was worth more than the truth. I remember being adored by girls who I never met before. It was a good feeling. I heard rumors about me that were not true. The myth was stronger than the man. People would exaggerate about some of the things I did. The exaggerations made me appear greater than I really was.

The downside to infamy is the effect it has on the police and potential enemies. The men I knew who had the biggest reputations are dead or serving long prison sentences. The police gather information on infamous criminals. The police use informants to learn about these men and women. The enemies of the infamous criminals will attempt to remove them or rob them. I can recall many violent conflicts and murders that occurred in Newport News. Most of them took place because of what one man thought about the opponent. If they both new the truth, they would both be alive. These incidents could have been avoided. How many men would still be alive if they did not spark fear in other people's hearts? How many men are in prison because of their reputation?

The concept of America's nightmare is reproduced over and over again through the media. It is birthed and rebirthed through the music. The thug idea is shared and reproduced by characters in movies. The things that are wrong become accepted. The masses begin to expect it.

The physical body is damaged by the behaviors associated with becoming a menace to society. Drug abuse and alcohol abuse accompany the lifestyle of a rebel. Sin kills the one who commits the sin. Our bodies suffer from the corrupt condition of the soul. People who develop unstable minds will show signs of instability on their flesh.

Altered Minds

Gang members tattoo their heads and faces to show their commitment to rebellion. Gang members get certain images painted on their hands and fingers to show their allegiance to a life of crime. One idea has altered their view of reality. What can make a man or woman want to join a team that is destined to kill its own members?

A man or woman does not need to belong to a gang to modify his or hers own body. Some people do it on their own accord. The television and social media present thousands of people who altered their own appearance. Common people are buying tattoos. Young men are placing rings and hoops inside their noses. I have seen many men and women placing metal in their lips, eyes, and tongues. Why are people not satisfied with their original appearance?

The women who appear to have little value for themselves pierce their bodies in places that are unnatural. Why? The young girls are putting rings in their noses and eyelids. I also see the piercings in eyelids and the cheeks. Why? Is it self-expression or is it self-hate? I believe there is a search for significance happening within the soul. The person who cannot find significance naturally may search for it in an unnatural state.

Television is used to redefine humanity. The music videos cause women to think that these new forms of body modification are acceptable. Mass destruction is not exclusively violent. Self-destruction comes in many different forms. Destroying one's own body is just one form. We are constantly taught that we are not good enough. We are constantly taught that we are not adequate. The biggest insult is in the context of money. We never have enough money.

The young men who don't see a future for themselves must understand that their lives do have value. The child who lives for God has value. The world will benefit from your positive impact. Your family and community will benefit from your talents and gifts. Women need to see a man who lives a righteous life. The children in the community want to see a righteous man. A righteous man proves that God is alive.

We must understand that we do have the potential of living a good, long life. The media shows us death and destruction every hour of the day. The music industry and Hollywood have the ability to produce a cloud to cover our minds. We have moments where we think God is dead. I meet people who do not think there is a God. Our minds have been perverted to the point where we think God is distant. God is not dead. Our inspiration is dead. Maybe our faith is dying.

God is Dead

Psalm 14:1 The fool hath said in his heart, There is no God. They are corrupt, they have done abominable works, there is none that doeth good.

The concept of God being dead was introduced in 1882 by Friedrich Nietzsche. Friedrich Nietzsche wrote a book entitled The Gay Science. The idea of living without God is appealing to people who want to feel comfortable living in sin. Friedrich Nietzsche was an atheist whose father was a Christian minister. At some point in his life, Nietzsche decided to prove that man can live without God.

The circumstances of his death proved that man cannot live without God. Nietzsche spent the last 11 years of his life in an insane asylum. Your soul will rebel against the body if you attempt to ignore God. This is the reason for the high level of perversion in the world.

I mention these facts because the teachings of Nietzsche have made a major impact on our lives. His teachings are presented in schools, universities, movies, and sitcoms. Instead of attempting to prove that no Creator ever existed: some philosophers want to believe that God is dead or no longer involved in this world's affairs.

The people who want to live hedonistic lives cannot do it alone. A hedonist must attract weak-minded to become hedonists with them. The people who profit from hedonism want to sustain the lifestyle. The Hedonist lifestyle is promoted in literature, universities, and through social media.

The Godless culture will be conceded on to the next generation if the good people do not offer an alternative. Wicked people must recruit others to share in their pleasure-seeking adventures. The good people must recruit others to be humble. Hedonistic people have a predatory attitude. They recruit through the media and learning centers.

The people who want to live without God cannot remove him from their lives. The people who hate God's supremacy cannot eliminate his presence. The alternative that settles their displeasure with God's presence is to alter his creation. The only way to remove God from the world is to pervert the creation that reflects his image.

The God haters must transform their belief in God or transform themselves. The multiple religions highlight the various beliefs in God. The new definitions of gender and roles reflects the attempt to alter the creation. Transhumanism is the scientific assault against God.

Humans cannot war with their Creator. God can remove our oxygen at any moment. God can stop a man's heart from beating just by making a decision. The atheists can only remove God's word from the public's sight. The God haters can only provide distractions.

Besides removing and altering the image of God. The men and women who want to live without God must distract themselves. The American culture consists of many methods of distracting itself from God. The nightlife is the most popular method. Every kind of adult works during the day.

The believers and the non-believers work day jobs. But the non-believers must find distractions during the quiet, serene nights. Music, television, nightclubs, and sporting events occupy the minds of pagans at night. The unsettled soul must stay busy with something.

All types of immorality are the result of the insatiable soul within a man attempting to please itself. It is not just the less fortunate people in the projects and the crime-ridden neighborhoods who oppose God. The wealthy and successful men and women live as if God does not exist. The educated professionals engage in immoral behavior just like the uneducated poor people. I did not understand how the rich and the poor were both lost until I moved to the Atlanta area.

The swingers, escort services, and foam parties were advertised in various publications. I also learned about the private clubs and exclusive movie theaters. The people with money are deviant just like the poor people. The rich are deviant on a different level. More money produces more options to fulfill larger fantasies.

God is not dead. That is impossible. God is not distant from his creation. Men and women choose to ignore his voice and they oppose his will. The people who want to remove God's authority have perverted his image and polluted his message. The children who are being raised in this current age do not have a lot of substance to maintain their faith in God. Many of the images of God are incorrect. Many of us are searching for a God that is different from what we are told. When I encountered the real God, I was confused. Jesus is not who I thought he was.

I believe that the children need to be exposed to the real thing. I also know that God will draw them at the proper moment. The people who deliver the message of God's Word are losing the respect and reverence of the citizens. God must do the work himself.

John 6:44 No one can come to Me unless the Father who sent Me draws him; and I will raise him up at the last day.

The religions who claim to know God reveal their flaws by making false claims. Christianity consists of more than 34,000 denominations. A denomination means division. If the Christians are divided, how can they restore a nation? If the Bible was written in Hebrew, why do we not know the Hebrew language?

The rebellious children and the confused adults do not have a lot of reasons to place their hope in religion. I meet people who don't have faith in God. I understand why they live without faith. I did not have faith in religion for a dozen years. The culture teaches us not to have faith in God. We are expected to fix ourselves.

The image of the world we adopt is one that consists of wicked, selfish men and promiscuous, deceitful women. This idea is imparted to us as young children. Hope can become a distant idea early in life. Some men and women rise above the negativity. Many of us do not.

We were told the only faith we can have is in ourselves and an idol we do not know. We idolize the people labeled as stars by the media. I remember worshipping athletes that I never met. The "God is Dead" movement allows people to ignore the Creator. The atheist movement allows men and women to feel at peace without God. That type of peace does not last. I tried it.

The peace that comes from ignoring God is not a true peace. That false sense of security is really a state of ignorance. The only way a person can live without God is to immerse oneself in frivolous activities. The people who want to remove God's influence attempt to redefine life. Good and evil must adopt new definitions to fit into a world without God. The atheists must present evil as good and good as evil. The other mind game is attempting to prove that there is no such thing as sin. If nothing is wrong then there is no right.

Nietzsche and other philosophers dedicated their lives to redefining the meaning of life. Sigmund Freud wanted to prove that guilt was not real. If Nietzsche can succeed and remove God from man's consciousness. When I was enrolled in college, I was introduced to many types of personality theories about human nature. These theories provide excuses for evil and selfish behavior.

I have been exposed to the teachings of atheists in college and in high school. These instructors and teachers have access to the minds of millions of people. The people they teach adopt the new world without God ideas. This is the reason many of us live our lives without acknowledging our Creator and don't even miss his presence. Our wireless, automated world keeps us stimulated and we don't stop to worship.

The results of living without God are manifested in our country. America has the highest prison population on the Earth. America has a high rate of rape and other sex crimes. The divorce rate is above 70%. Juvenile felons are increasing every year. Every nation has its own share of crime. But America is supposed to be different. We have the Bible and freedom to practice religion. We have disposable income and a surplus of food. We should not have crime, disease, divorce, and abortion at such a high level.

America has the most Christian churches on Earth. America has the most Christian pastors, teachers, and ministers. America has the most Christian rappers and Christian rock bands on Earth. Thousands of Christian authors live in America. Why is this country becoming more and more corrupt? Maybe the believers are living like God is dead. Maybe the Christians who claim to be Christians are not real Christians. Those of us who are real must do the work of the apostles. This world is getting worse.

If God is not dead, why is my life a mess? If God is not dead, why are the wicked people living in luxury? If God is alive, why do we endure so much tragedy?

When I was dealing with these philosophical questions: my mind was still enduring the torment of preparing to die before I reached the age of 21. I was 17 years old when I arrived at Barrett Juvenile Correctional Center. Being incarcerated was a waste of my time but prison is viewed as a rite of passage according to hip-hop and the street code. (We adopt some of the most stupid ideas ever known to man.) I was not ashamed of being incarcerated, but I knew I should be doing something more productive with my life. My soul was craving harmony and balance. How do I achieve harmony and balance if God is dead? Now I know he is not dead. I need to fix myself.

Hypocrite

I keep mentioning the idea of God being dead because most of us live as if God is dead. The religious people live like God is dead. I know many Christians who don't obey their own Holy Bible. I met Muslims who don't obey their Quran. The Mormons and the Jehovah's Witnesses have religions that appear to be fundamentally flawed. People live like God is not present and attentive. Men and women redefine God to fit their belief window.

I attempted to subscribe to several different religions, but they did not provide the harmony and peace my soul desired. My mind can accept anything that sounds good. My mind can accept a well-packaged lie. But my soul knows the truth. No human should ignore his or hers conscience. If something feels wrong, maybe it is wrong. Investigate.

The hypocrites are polluting the minds of the children. The hypocrites are providing terrible examples for the children. The lack of righteous fathers creates immature and deviant sons. The women who are irresponsible mothers create daughters with weak minds who become sex symbols and sex objects. Many of these boys and girls attend church every week. I was one of them. I learned how to lie from attending religious functions. Deviant and immature people search for deviant and immature leadership. Why not search for God? I was never satisfied until I found God.

The church culture may teach children how to be deceitful. I learned hypocrisy from acting like a good boy in front of church folk. We all learn how to act proper while people are watching us in church. We would commit our sin in secret.

The adults were the instructors. The way adult use their words is wrong. Never tell a child to act proper in public. Teach a child how to behave in private and that child will behave properly in public. Teaching a child how to behave in public will produce an alter ego in private.

The idea of acting proper in church reinforces duplicity. A man or woman should behave the same everywhere. Unfortunately, the religious adults were hypocrites. Children do what they see. I never teach my children how to act. I take the time to shape their character.

We need Godly role models in church. Not directors who teach children to look good. If a person can find one Godly role model, he or she should become that person's disciple. It is hard to find good leadership. So many men and women are compromised by sin. The direction that these people offer will be corrupted.

The homosexuals are also clouding the judgment of children. How can a gay man teach a child to do what is right? The gay man does not understand what is right. An immoral person cannot teach another person how to behave properly.

The only way a person can teach a child the difference between right and wrong is with a moral law. The moral law comes from the one who created morality. A person who chooses to live a righteous life will be in accord with God.

Gay men and gay women want justice and equality but they live in disobedience to God's word. Justice and equality were introduced by the Creator. Homosexuals are hypocrites because you cannot live in dysfunction and be good. Jesus said that the blind will lead the blind. The blind will lead the blind; straight into a ditch.

Luke 6:39 And He spoke a parable to them: "Can the blind lead the blind? Will they not both fall into the ditch?

I had trouble understanding who had the authority of determining right from wrong until I met people who submitted to the will of God. I always believed that no man had the right to tell another man what to do. I witnessed too many double standards. I met too many fake people.

The hypocrites polluted my worldview for many years. The fake Christians were the ones who did the most damage to my worldview. I was surrounded by church people as a child. The people close to me did the most damage. I met hypocrites on my football team. Players who envied teammates. Coaches who could not coach. Teammates who wanted to see each other fail. Hypocrisy is not just in the church. It can be found anywhere.

Hypocrisy is basically living a lie. The person who lives a lie damages the lives of those that they come into contact with. The hypocrite wants others to hurt the same way that he or she hurts. Hypocrisy is the act of not being what you claim to be.

I was a hypocrite. I was able to enjoy living as a hypocrite because I was surrounded by other hypocrites. Being fake only became uncomfortable when I attempted to behave as the real me. Then my associates hated me for changing. Hypocrisy is cool until someone decided to be honest. Hypocrisy is cool as long as each participant supports each other's deviant state.

We learn that God may not be who he claims to be by watching the adults who claim to believe. If a person claims to know the Creator, he or she should display signs that there is a relationship between him or her and the Creator. When a child lives in the presence of an adult who obeys the Word of God completely, that child will have a fortified faith. A parent who knows God and obeys God will protect and cleanse his or hers child's mind. The lies that child is exposed to will be uncovered and removed. Parents must remain in communion with God at all times. That is the only way a mother and a father can thoroughly protect the children.

The lack of honorable parents reinforces the God is dead attitude. I meet hundreds of people who don't have good parents. These people don't respect authority and they don't fear any spirit they can't see. The lack of a solid family structure adds to the decay in faith.

When an inmate returns home, how will he maintain his faith without a family that lives by faith? The children who are not incarcerated get indoctrinated into a mindset of Godlessness by their families. When a child leaves home to go to college; what is his or hers view of God?

Every life is a message. What message is your life sending? If you are a parent; what do your children think of God?

America's nightmare reincarnates itself because the culture loses its faith in God. We become more corrupt in our thinking. A corrupt mind leads to corrupt actions. A corrupt man corrupts a good woman. The corrupt woman corrupts the pure child. A cycle of destruction is generated. This cycle is triggered by one idea. "God is dead. Do what makes you happy."

I attempted to live like God was dead. I was living for myself and enjoying myself. These moments never lasted long. The Creator would find a way to invade my life. Men sink into deep darkness to evade the presence of God. We attempt to escape.

True learning begins at the edge of becoming uncomfortable. God made me uncomfortable to teach me lessons I would not learn while I was comfortable. The best laid plans will be sabotaged if God does not approve of them. I finally realized that Jesus is God; and He was real and present in this world. He reveals himself to truth seekers and his people. Jesus is alive.

Psalm 64:9 Then everyone will be afraid; they will proclaim the mighty acts of God and realize all the amazing things he does.

Atlanta

I moved to Georgia because I wanted to start my life over. I wanted to see something new and different. My life became better but I carried my problems with me to Georgia. The problem was my heart. The problem was not my address.

I was incarcerated for selling drugs in Atlanta in 1999. That weekend taught me a valuable lesson. My address changed but my heart did not change. I believe that I was compelled to move to Georgia for self-preservation. When I arrived there, I had dreams to accomplish something noble in my life. The problem was my unethical mind and my fractured heart was still out of order. I continued to find trouble and cause my own demise. The first enemy was the man in the mirror.

I moved to Georgia to live with my brother. One of the first things he did was take me to Georgia Perimeter College. A wise man would have enrolled in school following that visit. I had a chance to get a higher education but I did not follow through with that plan. My mind was not ready to do the right thing. My depression followed me to Georgia. My fears and insecurities were still present.

I did since a shift in my life but I had no power to make the necessary changes. A weak man needs courage or desperation to begin college. Weak men also need strong men who can sense weakness in other men. I wish I had a mentor to walk me through that process. I had dozens of older, negative men giving me drugs. But where were the positive role models? Sometimes I wonder if good men lack courage.

One of the major issues that plague men who lived a rebellious life is the easy access to vices. A former addict can find any drug he wants in any city. A former alcoholic can find a liquor store and another alcoholic in any city. A man who previously sold drugs will attract another drug dealer anywhere on the planet. This law of attraction appears to be a truth and not a myth. I always attracted the type of person I was at that time.

For a season I attracted scholars. For a season, I was surrounded by drug addicts. For a season I was surrounded by criminals. For a season I attracted promiscuous women. For a season I attracted depressed people. For a season I was surrounded by body builders and athletes. We attract the type of person we are. Who do you attract?

Proverbs 13:20 He that walketh with wise men shall be wise: but a companion of fools shall be destroyed.

When I moved to Georgia, I developed friendships with all the wrong people. I found all the drugs I wanted almost immediately, when I moved to Georgia. I did not need my brother to get drugs and alcohol. The negative vices are always available. I was even exposed to vices that did not interest me. Atlanta has a dark side that did not exist in Newport News in the late 90's.

Atlanta had a club for every type of sin and delight a man could imagine. Friends and co-workers would show me these places. I found some of them by chance. I thank God I was sober enough to leave these places. I am still amazed how easy a person can ruin his or hers life. But a man must use all of his energy and resources to do what is right. The same energy used to enter into sin is the same amount of energy that is needed to exit out of sin.

If a man or woman walks away from a vice immediately; he or she will not be trapped. But if a person does something that he or she knows is wrong for a long period of time: he or she will be trapped for a long time.

I felt the struggle of attempting to do the right thing. The negative acts are easy to commit but the positive acts require extreme effort. When my brother drove me to Perimeter College I spoke to a financial aid representative. She handed me a stack of papers to complete. I viewed the paperwork as an obstacle and not an opportunity. I did not need any paperwork to get high or buy alcohol. I never understood why the effort to do wrong is easy but the desire to do better is extremely hard. I never completed the paperwork necessary to attend Perimeter College.

I read many articles and books about traps being set to prevent men from changing their lives. I cannot prove that these traps are intentional. But I can speak from experience and state how hard it is to get ahead in a positive manner and how easy it is to remain a slave. Whenever I wanted to do something good; dozens of obstacles appeared. At times I just assumed I was cursed. Other times I believed I was not good enough to succeed.

I was a free thinker. I am an iconoclast. We are a people who want to succeed on our terms. It is not a negative trait. It is an independent characteristic. A freethinker can become a negative person if he or she does not have discipline.

A recollection from 1997 reminds me of a decision I made under extreme pressure. I was also alone when this incident took place. When I arrived home from Abraxas House; I was scheduled to be released from parole the following Monday. I arrived home the previous Friday. My parole officer told me that I could go to college if I remained on parole. I did not want to remain on parole but attending college was a good idea. This moment was intended to be a turning point in my life. The turn should have been a positive turn. I decided to get released from parole instead of accepting the help from the state. This decision is one I regret.

I did not accept this gift because I did not want to remain on parole. I wanted to be off parole because of my view of freedom. I thought I was free if I was released from parole. I did not have a mature view of the world at that moment. I just wanted to be free of the justice system. I knew that I may violate my parole while attending college. I still had the same friends and the same negative attitude. We were all smoking weed and drinking under age. I knew I would fail drug tests and probably violate curfew. A parole release was more valuable at the time.

I mentioned this incident because I know how hard it is to change the direction of your life. Life appears to be unfair. The cost to do right is always uncomfortable. The irony of this truth is that committing crime comes with a price. Every decision has a consequence. I did not enroll in college until 2009. It took me 12 years to do what could have been done then. I can only imagine how different my life would have been by now. I earned a Bachelor's degree in 2013. I could have had two PHD's by now.

Hundreds of clubs, strip clubs, pool halls, and bars exist in the Atlanta Area. These businesses keep men and women from knowing God. These businesses allow people to feel temporary pleasure every week. These temporary highs prevent men and women from feeling the need to change. The irony of these establishments is that they are usually populated with people who go to church every Sunday.

I know for a fact that my life would still be out of order if I never left Newport News. The acceptance I received from family and friends would have made me feel comfortable in my misery. I have a theory. If God does not upset the soul, none of us would seek change.

Transforming my life was not easy. I did have a lot of motivation to change. In the midst of the madness I encountered in Atlanta, I met a lot of women who did not like thugs. I met women who hated rap music. I also met young men who did not smoke or drink. These positive people were not religious either. They were just looking for a better life. These people encouraged me to search for something better for myself. These positive people kept me from giving up.

I had some moments that caused me to doubt myself. I had some moments of extreme frustration. The anger, confusion, and bitterness I felt was driven by the music I played. The negative messages were constantly repeated into my mind. The doubt would be based on the inspiration God put in me conflicting with what the world said about me. God said I was his disciple. The world said I was a failure who was supposed to use and abuse drugs. God said I was a teacher. The world said I was drug dealer who uses and abuses women.

The world distracts men from God and attracts them to drugs and wicked music. The most confusing aspect of my teenage years was the fact that I did not fit in with the religious people because I was too genuine and honest. I also did not completely fit in the streets. I was too truthful and honest. Too many fake people are in the churches. Too many fake people are in the streets. I understand why the young men and the young women are upset. Everything and everyone appears fake.

The illegal drug business is designed to destroy a man's life. When I was immersed in the illegal drug environment, I thought that was the easiest way to live. Live fast and die young. That sounds like a great idea to someone who does not want to live. The truth is most of the people involved in the illegal life do want to live. Extreme circumstances reveal the will to live. I met many former drug dealers in Atlanta. I worked with a few former drug dealers. All of them had remorse and regret.

The music, the dress code, the language and the atmosphere we generated made us believe we were supposed to be hip-hop and live the street life forever. My experience in Atlanta showed me there is more to life than impersonating hip-hop artists and living the life of a gangster we saw in a movie. Atlanta showed me that most of the entertainment business is designed to create a fantasy world outside of Disneyland. The whole rock and roll and hip-hop culture is used to keep adults in suspense. None of it is real. The suspense keeps people happy because it distracts them from their true condition.

Growth

The times I visited Newport News from Georgia, I wanted to fit into the same cliques that I walked with in high school. The reality is that no one can continue to fit into a group and grow as a person. No man can fit and grow at the same time. The work required to fit into the group prevents self-improvement and mental growth. Remaining a part of a group prevents you from looking outside the group for education, identity, and elevation. People have a habit of finding significance from their friends. The fear of losing a group of friends can postpone development.

If you want to grow, you will be required to let go of your former clique. Every member of that group will not want to change and mature. Letting go of the old friends is a challenge because you will feel insignificant. The fear of being alone in this world is enough to prevent a man from leaving his gang or clique. Your position in the world is dependent on those old associations. Generating new friends requires courage and risk. This is how we become a slave to our past. We must be taught how to live for the future.

A slave mentality is derived through years of indoctrination. Childhood was meant to be a carefree paradise. Our culture has transformed the carefree paradise of childhood into a worry-filled nightmare. A man does not become an alcoholic or drug addict in one day. The anxiety and panic that produces the desire for self-medication begins at an early age. The people who mutilate their own bodies did not make that decision in one day. The need for pain and extreme measures of excitement were caused by distorted emotions from the past. Unresolved emotions lead to absurd behavior.

We are indoctrinated into our negative, self-destructive behaviors by other men and women who exist in a state of depression. The people who immerse children into a world of fear and uneasiness were nurtured the same way. This toxic upbringing is passed on from one generation to the next. Adults whose lives consist of misery and sadness envy the children and young adults whose lives are full of joy and love. I had my positive dreams and optimistic views destroyed many times. The Christians destroyed by hope more than anyone else did. I started to believe I would never accomplish anything in my life.

We are taught that our lives should be lives of pain, disappointment, and worry. The media, negative peers, and some religions teach us to expect lack, derision, and distress. The news channels flood the airwaves with stories of rape, murder, and terrorism. This mindset will send a person in the wrong direction. Instead of thinking about prosperity, self-improvement, and how to succeed in life; we begin to plan for disaster. We begin to live in terror. We become slaves to fear. We begin to worry about events that never occur. This is an unhealthy state of mind. The Bible states that we must fear not over 60 times. I believe the media is being used to contradict the Creator.

Broken

When a man or woman develops an unhealthy state of mind, he or she will begin to develop unhealthy friendships and unhealthy allegiances. A whole, healthy person will seek the company of other whole, healthy people. A broken, depressed person will seek the company of other broken, depressed people. Once a person is mentally unhealthy, sound reason escapes his or hers life. Wicked behavior becomes normal behavior.

I Corinthians 15:33 Do not be deceived: "Evil company corrupts good habits.

Wickedness is the misuse of any idea, item, or substance that you did not create. Wickedness is the intentional abuse of the mind, body, and soul. The broken hearted lead lives of wickedness because of the weakened condition of their hearts. Good ideas are discarded and bad ideas become good ideas. Wicked people also recruit others to sustain their sinful lives. Sin is not exciting when it is committed alone.

The men and women, who are depressed and broken, congregate together with other men and women who are broken. The broken spirited men and women attract each other. People do not attract the type of people that they want into their lives. You will attract the type of person you are. This attraction is also the antagonist that prevents change. The broken hearted people want to remain with the broken hearted people. The broken hearted people do not want to survive alone. When your restoration begins, your current friends will attempt to stop it from happening. Your change will reveal their need to change. If you are successfully restored, they will need to be restored.

The desire for company and companionship compels the broken hearted people to stay broken. When one of the broken hearted attempts to fix his or herself, he or she will stop if all of his or hers friends cannot accept the change. When one of the broken hearted people attempts to share his or hers ideas for change with others who need to change, the ideas will be met with hostility. The broken hearted people do not want to lose one of their members.

A damaged person will attempt to stop another damaged person from becoming whole. The idea of being whole again produces fear. The fear of change is paralyzing. The slave mentality makes a person believe that he or she is weak and worthless. This attitude becomes comfortable. This attitude places no demand on the individual.

The streets are very attractive to boys and girls who lack direction. The lost boys connect with other lost boys. The insecure girls connect with other insecure girls. The weak boys and girls gather together with other weak boys and girls. The predators attract other predators. The streets are a place to find ones identity. This opportunity to find ones identity should be a positive opportunity. The reason this moment of choice becomes negative is the lack of proper mentorship. The negative elements of the streets are always near. The positive elements appear far away.

Galatians 3:26 For you are all sons of God through faith in Christ Jesus.

Identity

The child who is searching for his or hers identity may be confused, misguided, and unsupervised. This child is looking for a place to find peace and direction. A teenager who is confused, misguided, and unsupervised is prone to make bad decisions. This teen may find his or hers identity in the local gangs, cliques, or alternative religious group. The slave mentality is further ingrained because the lost teen will become the servant of any peer group he or she joins. He or she will become a servant because he or she wants to become a member.

Membership to a group, gang, or peer group will further induce weakness. A person who wants to become a member of a subculture must adopt their ways, manners, and belief system. No one can remain an individual while a member of a gang. A person who joins a subculture cannot expect to change it. He or she must change to join. This leads to an already depressed and disillusioned teen to become something even further away from his or hers true self.

The longer he or she remains a part of this subculture or gang, the more he or she departs from his or her true nature. Eventually, he or she will maintain this new false identity forever or become extremely paranoid. The paranoia is one of the symptoms of being disconnected from God. Extreme paranoia leads to self-medicating and self-mutilation. Some doctors may label this paranoia as a mental disorder.

A man or woman with a slave mentality will be unable to find his or hers true identity. The loss of identity leads to mental disorders. A person behaving outside his or hers intended design will begin to malfunction. Self-medicating and self-mutilation are examples of malfunction. No one in a sane state of mind will deface their bodies. No one who honors his or hers body will poison it. When a man pierces several areas of his face, it is because he does not want to recognize the image he sees in the mirror. When a man tattoos his neck and face, he is not functioning properly. Most mental disorders are the result of not being in communion with the Creator. If you do not know your maker, you will not know yourself.

The false identities we develop lead us into immoral behavior. Our false identities are sometimes self-defense mechanisms. We develop nicknames and hide our true feelings. We develop nicknames and behave one way in the schools and another way with our families. We have a different character that we perform with the opposite sex and another character designed for the Internet. Most of us have three or four people living inside of our minds. Our God designed us to only have one personality.

I did not find my true personality until years after submitting to God. I needed years of teaching and correction to realize how much of my persona was unnecessary and artificial. The man who wants to change must be willing to admit how fake he is first. The real you is the identity God established for you in the beginning. The fake you is the character that is contrived from the images we see on television and the image we create for our friends. The fake you is the image and reputation manufactured from your environment.

The challenge of identifying the fake you is that it may be a positive false image. The alternate persona can be the result of implementing a self-defense mechanism. Living in a stressful environment may cause a person to develop a separate self who can wipe away the pressure. I had a self-defense mechanism that allowed me to forget the extreme stress I endured. I could not handle the tension in my mind and soul. I also did not know my Creator.

James 1:8 A double minded man is unstable in all his ways.

Restoration takes time because all of the characters must be identified and removed. Restoration prevents these characters from returning. Our minds must be stable and sober. Clear thinking is essential to surviving in this world.

Multiple Personalities

The multiple personalities that we live with create situations that produce more trouble than we can manage. The multiple personalities attract various groups of friends. These friends invite you to do things that you probably don't want to do because you may not be in the mood. These personalities cause strife in marriages because a person married a character inside their mate. How often do men and women reveal their true demeanor before a commitment?

The personalities that we create allow us to fit into certain environments. I had a different personality for every social arena that existed in my life. I had a character for church, school, home, my place of employment, and my neighborhood. Each character was different than the other. This multitude of characters was created to allow me to please everyone. I was never happy though. No one attempted to please me. The goal was to be what everyone else wanted me to be.

Isaiah 26:3 You will keep him in perfect peace, Whose mind is stayed on You, Because he trusts in You.

The multiple personalities cause a lot of drama because they allow you to deny responsibility. When a person gets arrested for a serious crime, he or she will immediately declare innocence. The other personality is innocent, but it was the criminal personality who committed the crime. How many men and women swear that they were out of their minds when they committed a crime? How many people have hurt someone they loved in a state of panic or a passionate moment? Women often have sex and regret it later. I experienced this type of confusion many times. I don't remember some of the things I did and some of the hurtful words I spoke. Sometimes I do not remember my old friends.

One of the worst side effects of having multiple characters existing within your mind is the emotional highs and lows. A term used by medical professionals is manic-depressant. The multiple characters produce a wide range of emotions in a short time span. A moment that should produce joy may produce pain. A painful moment may produce happiness. I still remember laughing when I was arrested. I still remember the extreme fear I felt when I was told that I would be released in two weeks. How do I explain that? I should have been sad when I was arrested and overjoyed to get out.

The fear of leaving prison is enhanced because we know that upon release, we will have to feed all of the personalities living on the inside. We will also be pulled in several directions at once. The negative peers we were separated from while inside will be there when we get home. It is hard to say no to our former friends. We will also have to live up to the past reputations we earned. I remember days that I was afraid to go outside. I did not know what I might do.

The only relationship that must be maintained is with God. But that is the relationship that will remove our false identification. The removal of all false identification is akin to murder. We built our lives on the false identity; it will be painful to relinquish that reputation. The old slave man must be destroyed in order to become a new man.

No man can become a king with a slave mentality. The old methods used to sustain your life must be removed to produce new life. Everything that led to my incarceration, I had to identify and dispose. I cannot surround myself with the same people and expect a different result. I cannot surround myself with slaves and expect to become a king.

That type of miracle only happens in the movies. In the real world, a man must go through a lengthy process of attitude change and mind renewal to become righteous.

A king is someone who understands authority. A person who has authority is someone who understands and accepts responsibility. A king is also a person who understands ethics, morality, and diplomacy. A good man will promote unity and encourage other men and women to obey the law. The king that I am describing is a person who has control of his or hers own mind. The king that I am describing is a man who does not waste his talent and time. We must first gain control of own actions and our own thoughts before we can teach others. I cannot raise healthy children if I am not mature and developed.

I had to learn my true identity through careful study of the Bible. I began to understand who I was after reading the Books of Moses and the teachings of Jesus. I became a true man when I became a true disciple of the written Word.

My life and the condition of my children's lives improved when I recognized my true identity. My true identity is defined by God himself. I am to be his son. I am alive to reflect his nature. I am expected to be a Son of God. Jesus showed us all what we are supposed to become. Anything else is wrong.

Some of us spend most of our lives living as imaginary characters. We adopt these characters to hide the fears and insecurities that arise while becoming young adults. Some men adopt the street tough image we see in the movies. Some of us start to act like thugs because it provides a sense of strength and security when walking the streets. The tough image also attracts other young men who want to appear strong. Most of us don't know the cost of adopting this image and reputation. The longer a young man acts like someone he is not, the more he deviant he will become.

Behaving like a thug, pimp, hustler, thief, or a player was the slave mentality. These attitudes are immoral. These attitudes are not original. Becoming what God intended is original because there is only one of you. Being original is being what God designed you to be.

Controlling my lust and controlling my mind allowed me to display moral conduct. A true king controls his emotions and desires. A real man is not compelled by the music or the television to make decisions. A real man will make decisions based upon sound wisdom. Wisdom is shown by: being in the right place, doing the right thing, for the right reason, at the right time, with the right people. ' Purpose over pleasure' is a good rule to obey. Morality increases maturity. Morality is obeying God even when it is uncomfortable.

Colossians 3:12 Therefore, as the elect of God, holy and beloved, put on tender mercies, kindness, humility, meekness, longsuffering.

Morality

Morality is a concept foreign to teenagers and most young adults. I was not a person concerned with morality after the age of 13. I tried to maintain a moral lifestyle, but I allowed the culture to corrupt me. Morality is not presented to everyone as the foundation of living. The movies we watch contain immoral material. The music we listen to contains immoral lyrics. The people we come into contact with offer immoral options. Living a life of integrity and honesty is a challenge when the people surrounding you are not. Our culture allows a person to decide what is right and what is wrong by his or hers own definition. I see the damage caused by the culture in my children. I see the confusion in their faces when they do what is right and other people do what is wrong. Both of my sons were mistreated when they did the right thing. Redefining right and wrong is a form of idolatry.

The simple definition of morality is 'conforming to right and proper behavior'. Right and proper behavior is any action that does not violate purpose. Right and proper behavior is any action that does not violate a person or an object. Moral behavior is determined by the Creator. Wrong and immoral behavior is any action that violates the purpose of a person or an object. The intentional misuse of any idea, substance, or a person is wickedness. Immoral behavior is corrupt behavior. God is the one who decides what is right and wrong.

Psychologists and sociologists are not informing people of the difference between right and wrong. Most of them want to explain issues without Diving counsel. The social commentators on television want to make morality subjective. Many of the college educators and government officials attempt to define morality without the authority of God. This type of thinking allows people to choose what is right and wrong in their own eyes. Many psychologists do not speak about God's laws because they do not want to jeopardize their careers. Some of the unions and associations that they join prohibit the mentioning of God.

Anytime men and women are allowed to choose what is right and wrong, they will naturally choose whatever makes him or her comfortable. People must learn to be comfortable with the presence of God. Selfishness and pride reigns in the life of a person who only wants comfort. A man dominated by pride and selfishness will become immoral and separated from God. There is no morality without God's laws.

Morality is an issue that is always under scrutiny by people who want to redefine it. Morality is an issue that should not be under debate. We are all created with a moral compass inside of us. The conscience comes as standard equipment. Children know the difference between right and wrong. The adults definitely know right from wrong. The wavering of morality is usually based on consequences.

Children do not understand consequences. The adults violate human law and God's law as long as they can withstand the consequences. Sometimes adults will not stop their bad behaviors until they suffer a pain that is unbearable.

Moral issues are usually not complicated until someone complicates them. Abortion is wrong because it is murder. Rape is wrong because it is stealing. Drug abuse is wrong because it harms the body. Murder is wrong because it ends the life of someone who was given life by God. No one has the authority to take a gift from another person to whom they did not give the gift. Man is not God.

Man

What is a man? How should a man live? Who defines a man's role? These are just a few of the questions that I asked when I was a teenager. I needed to know my role on Earth. I needed to know why guilt was present when I was supposed to be happy. I needed to know why I was drawn to performing evil actions when I wanted to do what was right. What is a man? Why do I need to ask?

A man is a soul and a spirit living within a physical body. A man has a spirit that connects him to God. The man's body connects him to the physical world. The soul is the decision-making console within a man. A man is a soul. He lives within a body. The body does not define the man. The condition of a man's soul determines who he is. The soul makes all of man's moral and immoral decisions. The soul is the place within a man where his feelings, his thinking, and will power exist. The soul can choose to be good or bad. The choice is yours to make. The True and Living God does not make our decisions for us.

The man, who lives in communion with God, will have a soul that is at peace. He will know what God expects at every crossroad. The peaceful soul will avoid sin. The peaceful soul will want to know what God requires of him or her. The peaceful soul produces a confident and obedient man. The man who is at peace with God will obey his instructions and show others how to become an obedient and holy person. A holy man will have a positive impact on everyone he comes into contact with. The holy man is not outside the gate. He is in residence with God and experiences a sense of heaven while living here on Earth. He lives immersed with God's Holy Spirit.

A man is not what the popular media presents in music videos. A true man does not behave the way he is presented on television. Most of what is presented on television is propaganda and pure lies. The propaganda alters the view of the intended design.

A man was not designed to be a sex addict. A man was not designed to enjoy pornography. A man is not supposed to cover his body with ink. It is an act of wickedness to endure multiple body piercings. The only holes a man should have in his body are the holes he was born with. Any other holes are unnatural. Self-mutilation is becoming more popular because of the media. Tattoos are viewed as normal. The animal nature in a man should be tamed. The spirit in man should dominate the physical body.

A man was designed to know God and display God's character. The popular media presents man as a highly intelligent animal. The media is presenting humans as enlightened beasts. This is an intentional misrepresentation. As long as the social commentators can profile humans as animals, they can continue to justify immoral and wicked behavior. If the secular, social commentators were forced to admit God made man at a higher level than animals, the secular commentators would be required to teach and obey his commandments.

A man is much more complex than an animal. We were made in the image of God. Our true image is the image God planned for us when he created us in the beginning. Our births were not our beginning. Our creation at the beginning of time was our beginning. We should not confuse our birth with our creation. The modern, God-hating culture that exists in America has changed the image and the purpose of a man.

A man is more than a tax paying citizen. A man is more than a gladiator and an athlete. What we do to earn money is only a fraction of our existence. The contemporary culture has pushed men to live inside a small box. We have become a prisoner of our trades. We become slaves to our jobs and debts. A slave to debt is similar to living inside a literal prison. The man who is boxed into his job and bills is just as unhappy as the man boxed inside a prison cell.

The media misrepresents everyone. The street, thug image that we see on television is not an accurate representation of the people who live the illegal life. The real street thugs don't live the way we see them characterized in the movies. Too many teenagers get involved in the illegal life because of the apparent reward of money and freedom. The truth is that very few drug dealers and crime bosses survive the illegal life. Most of the real drug dealers will admit that they are not free. Almost every one of them dies young or is sentenced to a life in prison. God himself said that, "all sin will be punished." If the police do not arrest you, God will punish you.

I have known some drug dealers who were heavily invested in the drug game. These men showed me the dark side of the criminal life. There is no light side. It is a ruthless business. I have met some real murderers. Their lives were nothing like the lives we see on television. Guilt and shame tormented these men. These men would tell me to avoid getting deep into the business. I was always shocked to hear them warn me not to go too far. The ideas we have of life are mostly incorrect. I envisioned becoming a crime boss and enjoying the freedom and power. But the ones who lived that life were not enjoying the freedom and power. Guilt is real. God is real.

Our culture corrupts our minds. If you knew the truth about the end of the road you are traveling, would you still travel down that route? I am convinced that most of us are mentally unstable by the time we choose to live the illegal life. That is why we cannot be reasoned with. An unstable man cannot make a sound decision.

Culture

Genesis 6:10-12 And Noah begot three sons: Shem, Ham, and Japheth. The earth also was corrupt before God, and the earth was filled with violence. So God looked upon the earth, and indeed it was corrupt; for all flesh had corrupted their way on the earth.

The culture we live in is not designed to help young men and young women understand their relationship with God. The culture we live in is a pagan and materialistic culture. The people who hate God designed a world that produces children who are not aware that a God exists. The modern culture does not make room for an outside influence. The Bible states that the whole world exists in disobedience.

If the whole world is in sin; people must find a way to distract themselves.

The media is the medium that dwells between men and God. The media is the distraction people use to live their lives in peace. The time consumed watching television is the time that God gave us to communicate with him. The time we spend in the movie theater is the time we could be in prayer. The television and the music we listen to gives us visions and dreams that we should be getting from our Creator. The media is extremely clever in the way it disguises its purpose.

The true purpose of the media is to captivate the mind. The true purpose of the media is to impart propaganda into the minds of the viewer. We all live with wrong information in our minds. We all live with belief systems that are full of wrong information. I see many movies and shows that misrepresent God and his people. Most of the shows contain a message that suggests no God exists. The shows and movies that do incorporate the Bible present it wrong.

The media is currently introducing ideas that are hedonistic. Whenever a group, community, or nation develops a value system that removes God as the head; that community, group, or nation will become sinful. That sinful way of life will lead to rebellion, delusion, violence, perversion, and oppression. In the year 2013, we can all see the results of the sinful lifestyle we adopted. The wicked behavior the children adopt is taught to them by Hollywood and hip-hop. I am starting to see witches and Satanists in places that I never saw them before.

The media presents ideas that give teenagers reasons to rebel. The teenagers eventually rebel against their parents and other authority figures. Mass media is leading boys and girls to believe things that are not true. The men are behaving like women, the women are behaving with men. The perversion that is becoming normal is constantly shown on

TV. I see things that make me uncomfortable as an adult. I understand why the minds of the children are unstable. The biggest sign of the media's influence is seen in churches. The teenagers in church are adopting the lifestyle of the secular world. The music, speech, and dress code of the children of God should be different than the secular children.

Violence is increasing in schools and in homes. Violence has always been a part of society. The increase in school violence and domestic violence is a symptom of the lack of God's presence. The state and federal government becomes oppressive when the citizens lack ethics and morality. The violence is a symptom of the unstable mind. The physical outbursts and the uncontrolled emotions are the result of unresolved ideas in the mind. Suicide is a violent offense against oneself. Teenagers who choose violence are not thinking clearly. This is the predominant problem in the mind of teenagers.

Information overload is not a good thing. Especially when the information comes from many different sources. The music and the movies flood the mind with violent images. These images emerge at different times. The images emerge when the emotions change. The emotions determine when the images and ideas are recalled. The mind has little control over the recall of the things we receive through entertainment. Once the idea is implanted in the brain, only God can remove it from the memory. We must be born again.

The hip-hop religion is a major instigator of perversion. The hip-hop artists add to the delusion that ruins the minds of children. The lyrics that they write subconsciously implant messages that lead children on the path to self-destruction. The songs are implanted at a deep level within the mind. The listener is left on auto-pilot. The listener will voluntarily disintegrate on queue. A physical altercation may lead to a shooting because the idea is already in their minds before the conflict started.

State of Mind

Once a man is placed on a destructive path in his youth, he can be set on auto-pilot for the remainder of his life. He will self-destruct on queue by reacting to pre-determined signals. The path of destruction is being developed by the people who control the media. This type of social engineering is designed to separate the weak from the strong. A weak person will fall victim to the subconscious messages. A strong person will ignore the negative images on television.

Social engineering appears harmless because propaganda is the only thing most of us know. The social programming appears to be normal because the media is a major part of our lives. We are introduced to television soon after birth. As babies, thoughts and ideas are implanted while the human brain is forming. Ideas are introduced before a child can know the difference between right or wrong. I have certain ideas in my mind that will never go away. Some of those ideas are evil.

I recognized the influence television has on a developing mind at eight years old. I lived without television for years. I lived in Germany from 1983 until 1987. When I did begin to watch television, I noticed the change in my subconscious thought patterns. I still remember the first time I saw a person die on television. It scared me. I was in shock for a few seconds. The mind is a powerful machine. We destroy it when we introduce false images and violent pictures.

I also noticed how television affected my emotions and mind strength. I would lose my ability to concentrate and focus on an idea. The more I was exposed to watching television, my desire to read decreased. The worst impact of the television is the way it tells people to think.

Most of my friends do not have the ability to carry a thought to the next thought. When I would attempt to talk about a philosophical idea or a future dream, they would stop me. Their minds did not have the strength to engage in disciplined thoughts. They lacked the intuition and inspiration to imagine ideas. The hip-hop artists and the media tell them what to think. Emotions would guide their thoughts. Their emotions are attached to certain images.

Brain dead people need something visually stimulating to ignite conversation. Every moment has to be more exciting than the last moment. The mind cannot develop ideas and generate conversation because something on the outside needs to ignite them. I call people who live like that "zombies". The need for emotion and excitement produces a state of mind that prevents people from learning how to think. The physical urges begin to dominate the mind.

The mind can become inebriated by the constant stimulation it receives from external sources. The mind must be sober to handle stress and unexpected events. The mind must be sober to know the difference between a friend and a foe. The sober mind can control a man's emotions when he is under extreme pressure. A man must remain sober.

The ability to think is essential when leaving prison. Thousands of decisions will be made every day. Each decision leads down a new path. The decisions must be made without emotional stimulation because the consequences are real. I made many bad decisions when I was released because of how I felt about my friends. I made many bad decisions because my pride convinced me to impress women. If I operated with a sober mind, I would have ignored my pride and placed my loyalty in better people. If I was sober I would have used wisdom instead of emotion. A sober mind is a defense mechanism. A sober mind is a life preserver.

Our minds must remain strong. The mind is designed to produce its own thoughts and receive external ideas. The new technologies and the media decrease the mind's ability to generate original thought. Reading is an action that should be promoted more. Many times we recall an old thought and label it a new thought.

Mental stamina is important in this chaotic world. Every day will consist of new conflicts and new problems that must be solved. Without mental stamina, a man and a woman cannot maintain a marriage. Stamina is needed because people who need help will come to you for assistance when they see that you have strength. Reading and prayer increases mental stamina. Physical exercise also increases mental stamina.

The label ADD and ADHD are not always accurate. Some of the people who receive this label are not unstable. The people who receive this label are prescribed drugs. The drugs are expected to help a person think and concentrate. The truth is that these drugs damage the patient. These drugs produce many other issues. Almost every school shooting was committed by a student who was taking prescription medicine. I believe ADD and ADHD are not negative states.

Some people are hyper because they are naturally creative. Some people receive inspiration differently than others.

Delusion

Delusion is a false belief system. Delusion is caused by a person who wants to accept a truth because it provides comfort. The person suffering from the delusion has a lot of evidence that may prove his or hers belief system is wrong. But this person will not submit to the truth. The delusion provides peace. The truth will cause pain because change is uncomfortable.

Many of the teenagers I grew up with suffered from delusion. I was in a state of delusion. We believed that we were invincible. We believed that we could outsmart the police. We believed that we could break all the rules and still win. We also chose to accept the lie that our problems were caused by everyone else. We never accepted responsibility for our own decisions.

The misconceptions we lived with came through the media and older people who gave up on their dreams. When I was locked up, I never had a positive conversation about the future. The view we had of life was not optimistic. The conversations we had were about how to make more illegal money. The view of life we shared was the same view our favorite rappers talked about. We took their words and made them ours. The hip-hop artists became the social commentators when we lost faith in the religious leaders.

Our delusion remains a powerful one because the music is portable. The car stereo and the cd players allowed us to take the negative messages in the music everywhere we traveled. I still remember the feelings that I had whenever I stepped out of my car. I would be in a selfish and bitter state whenever I encountered a person. I learned to hate people who loved me and love the people who hated me. I refused to let powerful people help me because I thought that I was supposed to lose. A few times I quit at the finish line. I would show up for job interviews with a bitter attitude. The delusion insisted that I remain a slave.

The slave that I am mentioning is the person who submits his mind to poverty and foolishness. The slave does not want to improve his condition. The slave does not want to live an educated and liberated life. The slave enjoys incarceration because there is no demand placed on his life. No one expects anything great from a slave. The slave does not expect anything great from himself. The slave is always the victim.

When many people suffer from the same delusion, it becomes a subculture. Once we establish a subculture, we can develop our own rules and our own truth. The lies become facts and the delusion become real. Delusions are dangerous because the people suffering from the delusion will only surround themselves with other people who also accept the delusion. Subcultures create their own version of God.

The people who are suffering from the slave delusion and the street thug delusion exhibit certain behavior. The boys and men who sag their jeans and shorts are suffering from the slave delusion. There is no good reason to show your boxers and underwear. But these men feel comfortable doing it. Another symptom is the excessive tattoos. Men who don't know God have a twisted view of themselves. A twisted mind thinks the excessive body ink is an improvement of the creation God made. If God wanted my body painted he would have done it himself.

Another symptom of the delusion is childish behavior. Why do men behave like children? I see adult men who think that the world owes them something. I see adult men who cannot handle themselves anytime a demand is placed on their lives. Their childish behavior is a method of avoiding adult responsibility. These types of men do not want to support a family. These men want someone to care for them. A man who does not raise his own child is not a whole man. A man cannot raise a child if he is not responsible for himself. The obvious sign of childish behavior is a man who does not work every day. Every man should be making legal money somewhere. Some women exhibit childish behavior. A childish woman is a woman who chooses to have multiple children by multiple men. A childish woman collects welfare and does not work anywhere. This type of woman lives off of the government.

The delusional people isolate themselves from those who will not subscribe to the same fantasy. I remember becoming violent with the people who wanted to change my mind. I remember rejecting anyone who wanted to alter my way of thinking. I was in a delusion for so long it became a comfort zone. I knew that if I was separated from my delusion I would have to start my life over. What I did not know was how I entered into that delusion.

Violence

Violence is any physical force or exertion of power against an object, a person, or a group of people. Violence is a common occurrence between human beings. Violence is an action that men and women use against each other. Violence appears in many different forms. The form of attack may be verbal, physical, mental, or emotional. Some violent attacks are subtle. Some violent attacks are flagrant.

The men who choose violence as the first method of dealing with a conflict are men who lack wisdom, self-control, or integrity. These people lack something. I chose violence when I was under extreme pressure. Many of the fights that I engaged in could have been solved by talking. I also chose violence when I wanted to avoid the issue that instigated the conflict. Integrity will hinder violence because an honest person will not need to physically dominate another person. His or hers words have power.

Self-defense is natural. A man with courage will return physical force to repel physical force. The first attack is launched by the one who chose evil over peace. Violence became the norm in my life. My neighborhood had over a hundred teenage rebels. We fought and laughed all the time. In the beginning, it did not appear detrimental to my mental health. But just like any other sin or addiction; the violence became normal and expected. The so-called street life tolerates and expects violent behavior. Violence was the acceptable method of solving problems.

I had to fight to prove that I was a real man. The term 'real' and 'hard' were important during the early 1990's. Fighting was a way of getting street credibility. Fighting was the assumed rite of passage into manhood. The ironic fact about the middle and high school violence was the high rate of friends fighting friends. Most of the school fights were friends fighting people that they already knew. The fist fights that I engaged in with strangers were intense. I only had a few fights with complete strangers. We did not know if we were going to kill each other. Maybe that is the reason people avoid fighting complete strangers. How often do you see two complete strangers fight each other?

The music during the early 90's contained violent lyrics. Certain songs that were played during house parties would instigate fights. Certain songs that were played in night clubs instigated brawls. The music altered the listener's mind. Music is a mind altering substance. The subconscious mind receives instructions from song lyrics, and the listener responds with violent behavior. The listener may not realize that he or she has no control over his or hers response. I can remember hundreds of moments that I lost control. The music and the stress of the moment caused me to respond in a violent manner.

Genesis 6:5 Then the Lord saw that the wickedness of man was great in the earth, and that every intent of the thoughts of his heart was only evil continually

The current generation has a violent spirit. The evidence is displayed in the increase of mixed martial arts, popularity of football among women, youth mixed martial arts, and female boxing. Violence is not exclusive to adult males. Women and children are now participating in violent sports. The other sign of the fascination with violence is the blood and gore video games. Millions of children are captivated by violent video games. The blood and the dead bodies are not offensive to the viewer. The reward for killing is an incentive to continue playing the game. The high associated with the success of killing another character is addictive.

The love affair with killing is changing our nature. People only need a simple suggestion or a minor reason to kill. This must change. The triggers used to excite the players of video games transfer to reality. The kids who enjoy killing during video games will have a desire to kill real people. This type of programming must be recognized. The person who is programmed to kill must have his or hers mind renewed. A person who is incarcerated should have this attitude detected and adjusted before he or she is released.

Perversion

Psalm 73:6 Therefore pride serves as their necklace; Violence covers them like a garment.

Perversion is becoming an acceptable behavior. The public displays of perversion and debauchery were not accepted in the past. The general population is proving that we no longer live inside God's gate. Sodom and Gomorrah was destroyed because of the high level of wickedness on display. We must not approach that high level of wickedness.

Homosexuals hid their wicked behavior in the past. Gay people are not ashamed of their condition anymore. I have seen gay people display their deviance in churches. Young children will be conditioned to believe that homosexual behavior is acceptable. The truth about homosexuality may never become transparent. I had to search for the truth about this movement. Sex is not the main reason for these people declaring civil rights. These people want to redefine human existence. This is why they want to change the public school books.

Only three percent of Americans live the gay life. The entertainment industry wants people to believe it is closer to fifty percent. This lie causes men and women to think that they can cross over without consequence. The news networks show marches and rallies during news broadcasts. The goal is to make people believe the whole world is supporting immorality. That is not true. I always wondered how the wicked people gained control over the media. The media may have been wicked from the start.

The original intent of the entertainment industry was social programming. The original intent of the media was progressive brainwashing. The people who controlled entertainment wanted to oppose the religions that taught morality. The Christians have the power of God. The Pagans use the media.

Pedophiles are not mentally ill. Pedophiles are evil people. Pedophilia is currently being redefined as a mental instability. The truth is that pedophiles are evil people looking for a victim. An advocacy group in America is currently lobbying the federal government to legalize their actions. This is a sign that we are not respecting or obeying God anymore. These types of people are symbols of what men become when they flee God's presence. Pedophiles are predators. Sin has no limit.

The Bible also forbids men and women from engaging in homosexual relationships. Uncontrolled lust leads to forbidden love. God has rules in place that compel men and women to control their lusts and learn to be content. Sin has no limit. Perfection is limited. God gave us limits so we can progress to the next level of life. Whenever a person removes the barriers, he or she is redefining life. That person is attempting to become a God. It is a fact that most of our knowledge is wrong. What we call wisdom and progress is evil in the eyes of God.

Man vs. God

Proverbs 21:30 *There is no wisdom and no understanding and no words that can stand against the Lord.*

An excuse is an acknowledgement of an inconsistency. The reasons I have for making bad decisions reveal the defects in my own character. As a juvenile felon, I had many excuses for breaking the law. As an adult, I now realize that some of the reasons my friends and I lived the illegal life is because it was available. Some of the traps that destroyed our lives were placed before us. I am a believer that some of our issues were designed to hinder our development.

I do not believe that the destruction of my generation was a deep, dark conspiracy. I just believe that the destruction of my generation was caused by people who oppose God. The people who oppose God have positions of power and influence. These people use their influence to produce a community of non-believers.

I developed some of my opinions from my years in college and high school. I worked for people on several jobs who did not submit to God. I went to church with people who did not submit to God. When a young boy spends his adolescent and adult years surrounded by God-less leadership, he will develop a hard heart and an independent spirit. I forgot how to hear and obey God. I began to trust myself and oppose everyone else.

The people who hate God do not have to teach others to hate God. The only thing they need to do is promote comfort and independence. When a person begins to desire comfort and independence, that person will disobey God automatically. God haters will choose a form of God that allows them to control their higher power. Some of us resist God because our lives are too comfortable. The true God, Jesus, is not controlled. He controls his people.

The people that I am describing are school teachers, scientists, Hollywood executives, and music producers. We are exposed to people who don't believe in God early in our lives. I was influenced by religion at home. But I did not see the presence of God or his knowledge. Every now and then I sensed the presence of God but it was not by design. I never witnessed the presence of God during an incantation at a church. He would show up when he wanted to teach me a lesson. It was religion that I detested. I cannot admit to being a God hater.

The American culture tends to separate God from society. This separation allows children to live immoral lives five or six days a week and still attend religious meetings. I would behave one way in church and behave another way in school. The neighborhood I lived was full of church kids. None of us acted holy though. I really didn't know how to act as a child. I developed multiple personalities trying to please everyone. God was small. I was not committed to please him.

The people who helped destroy my generation gave us the tools to destroy ourselves. The mantle of freedom is also the chain of ruin. The ideas that people view as freedom are the same ideas that violate the laws of God. Many of our freedoms are the catalysts for our decay. We have religion in every community but a low amount of God's presence.

If America is a Christian nation, why is it not producing righteousness? We may never be perfect but we could have more unity. How many people are obeying God?

Proverbs 1:7 The fear of the Lord is the beginning of wisdom, but fools despise wisdom and discipline.

Abortion is labeled a freedom of choice. Abortion is an act that destroys a woman's conscience. The other freedom that assists young people with self-destruction is the freedom of religion. This freedom was designed to prevent the government from controlling the spiritual lives of its citizens. This idea has a new definition. The new understanding is that all religions are equal. The idea that any religion is good leads young men and young women into a realm of confusion. God becomes a mystery and loses his reverence as the Creator.

The most segregated time of the week is Sunday morning. The large numbers of churches in our cities add to the division. Most of the Christians I meet do not agree on simple truths about Jesus and sin. The freedom to choose my own church is a good idea, but that freedom produces private agendas and a lack of accountability. The children suffer because they may never know the truth of the Word of God. Thousands of different churches host thousands of meetings each week inside their walls. How many of these churches have men who walk the streets and serve the people in need?

I saw the effects of this religious division and confusion in my own family. Every member of my family belonged to a different Christian organization. This lack of unity caused doubt. I was constantly denying my Christian religion as a child. It was embarrassing to admit I was a Christian because of the way Christians appear in public. The lack of unity by the adults had a negative effect on the children. We all knew about God but no one knew God.

Wireless and Friendless

Isolation and individualism are two aspects of the deception of freedom. These two elements damage people. The freedom to use wireless technology has created a selfish and isolated society. The negative characteristics in a man are exposed when he has the resources to support them. The cell phone connects men and women to other men and women who really do not love them. The irony is that the cell phone disconnects people from God who does love us; while simultaneously connecting us to people who do not loves us.

The wireless technology that is poisoning our existence are cell phones, the internet, and Facebook. Cell phones allow us to talk to anyone we want without being in their presence. I am not ignoring their convenience, but we cannot ignore the danger. When a teenager gets immersed into the wireless world, he or she begins to lose the ability to fellowship with other people. I have met teenagers who do not know how to communicate with people outside their immediate social circle. I know teenagers who panic in the presence of people. Genuine relationships fail to materialize.

Ecclesiastes 4:10 For if they fall, one will lift up his companion. But woe to him who is alone when he falls, For he has no one to help him up.

The wireless world hurts the development of people's social skills. The lack of social skills plays a part in the high rate of criminal behavior. Boys and girls who don't have mature social skills will not know how to handle stress and opposition. The wireless world attaches people to who they want to be around. Character development requires the company of people you agree with and the company of people you don't agree with. I always had friends I liked and did not like around me. We chose to be friends even though we did not need each other. The idea was to be together and challenge each other. This new world has changed the dynamic of friendship.

Friendships are no longer mutual and genuine. Friendships are based on one leader surrounding his or herself with followers. The leader controls the other members of his or hers clique. The new technologies permit this type of egotistical living. The person with the biggest ego will only call people who can play a role for the moment. In the past, my friends and I did everything together because we did not have the ability to contact each other at any moment.

When I was a teenager the internet was not public. The only access we had to computers was during school hours. After school, my friends and I spent all of our time outside. Fellowship was the main thing. We would spend hours at the basketball court and playing football in the field. Personal relationships were important. We all knew how to build friendships. We all knew how to forgive each other. The people I grew up with were able to handle issues with other men and women. The kids I see today are not able to communicate. Many of them cannot handle stress.

My generation was not great at managing life and relationships, but the young people today are worse. My son goes to school with children who do not talk to each other. When I was in school, I could name every student walking the hallways. We were all connected on some level. The schools today consist of disconnected students.

The internet is allowing young people to sit in their homes and communicate electronically. The internet is also allowing people to communicate with people that they may not communicate with in person. The digital relationships are removing the need for character building. A person who only communicates through the computer will not be compelled to mature. The online persona is manufactured.

People who prefer to have online friends will feel perfect in their own skin. Humans were designed to grow through human contact and live community relationships. The internet relationships are mainly superficial. I always feel the need to look people in the eye when I talk to them. I would rather not have a friend than be united with someone who is fake.

Facebook is a computer program that connects men and women from across the globe. Facebook was designed to allow men and women to post pictures, send messages, and promote events. Millions of people use Facebook to present their lives to the internet public. This idea is good within itself. But the premise is based on healthy mature people.

I am beginning to believe that the majority of teenagers and young adults are not mentally fit. Facebook is becoming a site that promotes the wickedness in man. A researcher mentioned that over 60% of the profiles on

Facebook are false. Boys and girls are creating profiles of themselves that are not real. Young adults are also using the site to promote and share their immoral behavior. Evil people now have access to good people.

I forced my son to cancel his Facebook page. I did not want him to be exposed to the foolishness on that site. Too many teenagers are posting things online that they would be ashamed to present in public. The electronic tools allow teenagers to be vile and nasty to each other with no repercussions. My son does not need to be hurt by people who would never do it in person.

The wireless technology is designed to improve our lives. I use the internet almost every day. I own a smartphone that contains applications for Facebook and the worldwide web. I don't oppose technology at all. I am just mentioning the negative aspects of our culture that are the direct result of these technologies. Every invention has a consequence.

Technology adopts the characteristics of the user. I know adults who hate themselves. I meet teenagers who hate themselves. This hatred is transferred to the other people online. I remember being in chat rooms that were full of people who posted nothing but obscenities and gay comments. I also remember reading messages from men asking for underage encounters. I have not been in a chat room since 1999. I will never allow my children to enter one.

An adult and a child who cannot function in the real world should not be immersed in an electronic world. The mentally healthy people must return to forming personal relationships without wireless tools. The people who are not mentally healthy will never become healthy using wireless technology. I never thought that if was a coincidence that movies, who portray the lives of deviants, always show them sitting in front of a computer screen. The ordinary person has face to face friendships with his or hers peers. It is a lot harder to hurt and deceive people face to face. I want my children to develop face to face relationships.

Purpose

Four main ingredients are necessary to function properly in the real world. These four ingredients are purpose, goals, vision, and a plan. Each ingredient is found in the Bible. Each ingredient is necessary to maintain focus throughout each day of our lives. What is your purpose?

Isaiah 43:7 Everyone who is called by My name, Whom I have created for My glory; I have formed him, yes, I have made him.

One of the first feelings of lack comes in the form of purpose. I had trouble seeking a purpose for my life. I knew where my friends would be when I was released from prison. I knew where the available women would be when I arrived home. I knew where to go and get my drugs. I also knew where to find a job if I wanted to find employment. The challenge was finding a positive purpose for living.

What am I working towards? Why continue to sell drugs? What is the purpose? If I had my own house I would become a slave to a mortgage company. If I continue to hustle in the streets I may go to prison for ten years. I did not want these two outcomes for my life. I always ask young men about their plans for the future.

I did not want to become a man who worked every day to pay bills. That type of life was not appealing to me. If I wanted to live that life, I would not have become a rebel in high school. I was determined to never join the military. I had no desire to risk my life for a country I did not appreciate. I did not trust the military because many of the soldiers had no money. My only goal was to not return to prison.

Purpose is something that every man needs to find to fulfill his life. Purpose is the inner desire that inspires a man's will to survive. Purpose will also help a man direct his emotions and desires. Without purpose, a man will waste his time and his energy. Without a defined purpose to live, a man will have to develop his own drive in life. The drive men form is usually a self-centered one. We cannot carry other people if we do not know what to do with ourselves.

Whenever a man creates his own purpose for living, he also invents the rules. A man will subconsciously eliminate the presence of God. When God is involved in a man's life, the man no longer makes the rules. The main reason Jesus is opposed is because he invades our lives. Jesus Christ places a demand on his disciples. The Apostle Paul wrote that we were bought with a price. Our lives are no longer our own. The Book of Corinthians reminds the children of God that we are not owners of our lives once we have been born again. Our purpose is defined and determined by God. No other religion has a God who lives inside his followers.

The one who created us is the one who decides our purpose. The main problem associated with deciding our own purpose is the fact that we choose our purpose based on its reward. A man can miss his destiny by consuming all his time working toward a specific reward.

The reward may not satisfy a man's soul. Most of us get frustrated while working toward the reward. The frustration that is caused by defining your own purpose is the cause of many nervous breakdowns and family ills. Nothing will bring satisfaction except the presence of God in your life.

ESPN developed a documentary that highlighted the money professional athletes wasted. The title of this documentary is *Broke*. This show is just one presentation that highlights how our lives mean nothing without a relationship with our Creator. These athletes achieved their dreams and earned a lot of money along the way. When they reached the pinnacle, they discovered methods to destroy themselves. They did not realize their true purpose. They created their own purpose with their physical gifts. They threw away their wealth by attempting to create their own heaven. Money, power, and fame is no substitute for the presence and influence of God.

Finding Purpose

I had the opportunity to focus on spiritual things while I was incarcerated. The lack of media hypnotics provided me with time to think. I was not high, drunk, or distracted while I was incarcerated. I was frustrated with my condition and I was upset at a God I really did not know. Life did not make any sense to me in 1996. When I did what was right, I was ridiculed and punished for it. When I did what was wrong, I felt powerful but I was still eventually punished for it. Something is not right. I had to learn what was right. I also had to learn what was wrong. There can be no right without determining what is wrong. Who has the authority to decide what is right and wrong?

Psalm 119:10 Your word I have hidden in my heart, That I might not sin against You.

I read many philosophical books while I served my time. I read the whole Quran twice. I studied dozens of lessons from the Five-Percent teachings. I also read books about civil rights activists and politicians. I read books about the shadow government and the true concept of money. I wanted to know who God was and how did men respond to him. I wanted to know what my job as a man was. I read books about Bob Marley, Malcolm X, Frederick Douglas, Eldridge Cleaver, Donald Goines, and American History. I read many other books written by social commentators. Many of them were about Black men, Black history, and

I never read the Bible while I was incarcerated. I believed that it was not effective. I read it when I was a child and it did not appear to help me. Why read it again? I also noticed how it did not help those who professed to believe in it. The people who claimed to be Christians appeared to be walking contradictions. How can they live for another world without changing this one? Why not die as soon as you baptized? Their claims made no sense to us.

The Muslims appeared to have more credibility because they wanted men to be positive role models and discipline themselves. The Muslims did not tell everyone else they were going to hell for not praying to a White Jesus. The Muslims gave us a purpose for living now and a step by step process to perfection. The Christians wanted us to live for nothing and operate on a blind hope with no direction. It was easy for me to adopt a Muslim mindset.

Anyone who does not think that the images associated with their religion negatively impact other people are wrong. My friends and I developed a contempt for Christianity because of the pictures and paintings associated with it. The White Jesus and the naked babies flying around with wings made us uncomfortable. Why were all the angels' naked White people? I still remember the painting of heaven being a pedophiles fantasy. The painting showed two White men laying on clouds being fed grapes by two naked little boys floating with wings. These images will separate a child from the True and Living God. How can anyone subscribe to a culture that endorses these images and ideas?

All of the reading I engaged in was an excellent method of avoiding trouble. I was a model inmate. I only engaged in one physical altercation in eight months. Reading occupied my time. Reading also taught me how to think again. I was able to separate the image of a situation from the reality of the situation. I had enough wisdom to know how to ignore foolish people. A few men would make comments to upset me. They were afraid of a man they could not conquer. I did not fight all of them because they were not my enemies. They hated me. I did not hate them.

Sometimes incarcerated men react without thinking because of what they expect to happen. Your imagination and prejudice will rule you if you stop thinking. Every situation is not worth fighting over. Some enemies are a threat. Other adversaries are just jealous.

Reading books gave me the power to depress my imagination. Truth and logic began to reign in my thoughts and speech. These changes were great while I served my sentence. I did not have many choices to make in state custody. The information that I acquired is only effective if my character changed to good. A man's gifts are only valuable if he has solid character. The true condition of my character will be uncovered when I am released. All convicts claim to be good while incarcerated.

All of the learning in the world is wasted if it is contained in a wicked person. When I was released from Barrett I reclaimed my freedom. I suddenly had hundreds of choices to make. My true nature was revealed. I obtained a higher degree of knowledge, but my heart was still polluted. I wanted to continue reading, but my polluted heart attracted other forms of pollution. We don't attract the people we want into our lives. We attract people who resemble what we are. I attracted polluted people and I returned to polluting myself.

It was too hard to read and drink alcohol at the same time. I eventually stopped reading.

The reading stopped because I returned to my self-destructive behavior. A man cannot build and destroy at the same time. No man can plan for war and peace at the same time. I started smoking and drinking while living in Abraxas house. I was not concerned with religion or philosophy anymore. I just wanted to get high and find a new woman to conquer. My friends and I did not see a bright future for ourselves. The juvenile justice system prepared us for the adult correctional system.

The music we listened to reinforced our belief in opposing the system. We needed the music to remain angry. The music reminded us that we were supposed to be drug dealers and womanizers. It is easy to fall victim to negative messages when the people around you are negative. I continued to live in my past. I did not know I could start my life over anytime I wanted to start over.

2 Corinthians 5:17 Therefore if any man be in Christ, he is a new creature: old things are passed away; behold, all things are become new.

The difference between living for God and living for man is extreme. Am I living for tomorrow or am I living for yesterday? Yesterday I was depressed, oppressed, confused, and weak. Tomorrow I will be free, healthy, wise, strong, and full of joy. God prepares us for tomorrow. Men remind you of your past. God knows what you will become in the future. Men label you based on your past.

We always want to live in the past. Living in the past is easy because you know what happened. You can replay those painful events in your mind and choose how to manipulate the facts. You can use the past to excuse poor behavior in the present. The past is how we develop our identity.

God prepares us for the future. It is the future that frightens us. We don't know what will happen tomorrow. We have no control over the future. God gives instructions that we must follow to be ready for an event we have never encountered before. God teaches us things that we never knew existed. The new ideas and the new people God presents to us provokes fear in our hearts. When God gets involved in a man's life, everything is new. He is being prepared for tomorrow. I wish I knew this a long time ago.

I attempted to find a purpose in my life but those plans were derailed when I was released. I could not make the necessary changes without the influence of my Creator.

Goals

A goal is a dream with a deadline. A goal is the desired end result of a project or list of objectives. When a person fulfills his or hers goals; it builds hope and positive pride. I had trouble achieving my goals for years. I started to become depressed from all of the constant failure. I started dozens of projects and side businesses that were unsuccessful. Every idea I imagined I made an effort to bring to life. Almost all of my ideas failed.

The completion of goals justifies purpose. I learned what my true purpose in life was by acknowledging the fruit of my labor. The objectives that I completed with little effort were the areas of my natural gifts. The objectives that I had to achieve by lying, cheating, and stealing were not my naturally gifted areas. Any goal that requires a person to become a liar, cheat, and steal is not a legitimate goal.

I accomplished a few things easily. I earned my Associates degree with ease. I stayed in school and obtained a Bachelor's degree. College is easy for me. This is a sign that learning is easy for me. Writing is also a gift. I have no problem writing and teaching the lessons that I learn. I realize that learning, reading, and writing are my natural gifts.

Some life goals are short-term and some goals are long-term. The short-term life goals are the objectives that can be completed in a few weeks, months, or any term less than two years. A short-term goal can be seen from the beginning. An example of a short-term goal is planning to attend college. Another example of a short-term goal is fulfilling the required steps to get released from prison. Another example of a short-term goal is to gain employment. Obtaining my GED was a short-term goal I achieved when I was in Abraxas House. Another short-term goal I set and achieved was obtaining my CDL driver's license. I earned my CDL license in four weeks.

A long-term life goal is something that may not be seen from the beginning. Long-term goals require patience and planning. Long-term goals are fulfilled over an extended period of time. A Bachelor's degree is an example of a long-term goal. A Bachelor's degree is earned in three or four years. Another example of a long-term goal is planning to get married and support a family. Preparing for marriage and learning how to support a family requires planning. A person who is not preparing for a family ahead of time will not be able to support that family when it arrives. I was not prepared when I started my family. I had many problems to overcome. My wife and children had to suffer because I did not understand how to plan ahead. Another long-term goal is preparing for retirement. No one will work forever.

What long-term goals do you have? What do you want in five weeks? What do you want in five months? What do you want in five years? Goals provide motivation. Goals provide a reason to live.

Vision

Vision is one of the most important things a man or woman needs when being released from prison. Vision is the ability to anticipate the future. Vision is having a message statement, foresight, and a plan to fulfill your purpose. Each man and woman must have his or hers own vision. No one can give another person a vision.

The vision is what allows a person to maintain his or hers direction after a distraction. Vision is necessary because a person must have a set plan to avoid losing focus. Vision prevents the loss of focus. The lives we live are full of distractions. There will be times when friends and family members attempt to distract you from your goals. Vision prevents detours and disruptions. Vision is that element that will steer you back on course after losing focus.

The vision you have must come from within. Your vision must be internalized because it directs your path. The vision will determine who you share your ideas with. A man with a vision is a man who does not waste time, energy, or resources. The vision places a demand on the person with the vision. The internalized vision does not exit a person when life becomes difficult. A vision that comes from any source other than God or yourself may be an illusion.

An illusion appears real because you can see it. Sometimes you can touch an illusion. But it is still an illusion. The danger of being in an illusion is the time wasted attempting to apprehend the illusion. Some men waste valuable years of their life trying to fulfill dreams that God never intended for them to achieve. I spent three years of my life and thousands of dollars trying to be a hip-hop artist. I also wasted three years of my life attempting to be a drug dealer. These positions were not designed for me to fill. I could have used those years to write books and learn instrumental music. I learned the saxophone in 1996. I have not played the saxophone since 1996.

A man can be motivated by an external source. Money motivates people to work. Motivation is more external than internal. Vision is more internal than external. A friend or family member can tell you what to do and how to do it. A friend or family member can provide exhortation and encouragement. The impulse provided by vision will drive a man or woman to achieve his or hers goals with an extreme intensity. Vision will energize you when no one else is there.

Motivation is temporary and superficial. Motivation is a good instigator but it does not last. Motivation empowers the pride in a man. The soul needs more than a physical impulse or a visual incentive. Motivation only works while the motivating factor is present. Motivation can be diffused by the pain and discomfort of the work required to achieve the goal. I lost my physical drive many times. Whenever I thought the reward was too far away I would quit. Motivation is needed but it must be accompanied with vision.

Motivation is very effective for team activities. But the man or woman who is seeking to fulfill his or hers purpose needs vision. When I was going through my personal transformation I was alone for days. When you begin your transformation, you will be alone. Jesus wants you to only focus on him. Vision will help you stay on course. Time alone with God is healthy.

God will provide the plan that will help you survive inside his gate. He will also provide the plan of restoration that leads to salvation. His plan is perfect for victory in this life and preparation for the world to come. No one knows what happens after death. We only know that it will be better than this. The afterlife is an existence with God.

Plan

The plan for surviving outside the gate should come from the one who knows you the best. The one who knows you the best is the one who created you in the beginning. The one who created you in the beginning knows exactly what you need to be made whole again. The God who created you knew you before you were corrupted. God knows what your purpose is and he knows how to guide you into fulfilling your purpose. The method God will use to fulfill your purpose is perfect. Follow his plan.

Every man and woman will have a different plan. Some of the concepts involved in devising the plan may be alike. I can guarantee that no two plans are the same. No two people are the same. We all have different histories. We all have family histories that are full of tragedy, death, dysfunction and betrayal. The type of healing that is required for each man and woman is unique. The healing that I required was mostly mental. I was never sexually abused or addicted to any cosmetic drug. My mind was corrupted.

The restoration plan that the Creator establishes will heal every facet of your life. The world we live in damages many different parts of our lives. Restoration is not the change of your original nature. Restoration is the return to your pure original nature. The true and living God will not change your original traits. The return to purity is the removal of sin and shame. The traits that he put in you were supposed to be there. Our problem is the misuse of those gifts. The restoration process teaches us how to properly use our gifts.

The repair that we endure will teach us how to use our gifts in a positive manner. Criminals have a high amount of courage, teamwork skills, and organization. The True and Living God will teach us how to use these skills to do legal work. The sin nature used these attributes to steal, organize crime, and rob. We use our courage to break into houses and engage in street fights. Restoration does not remove the courage, teamwork skills, and organization. Our gifts will never be removed by the Creator. The repair plan redirects our energy into legal activities.

It would be wise to identify your attributes as soon as possible. What attributes are you misusing? What attributes do you use properly? A common list of attributes is: independence, strength, endurance, high tolerance for pain, courage, good speech, patience, discernment, good memory, athleticism, good math skills, and compassion. If you have a colorful imagination you can develop a comic book. Each one of these character traits can be used for good or evil. The plan of restoration will show you how to do what you were designed to do from the beginning.

Every child of God is not expected to be a preacher in the church. Some of us are designed to be disciples outside the church buildings.

I remember a couple friends I was locked up with who do not have any parents. These two teenagers were taking care of themselves. They were both sons of drug addicts. The plan God institutes for them will be different than the one he instituted for me. The feeling of neglect that results from not having parents will make it hard for a child to trust God as father. These men will need to learn lessons that are painful. Restoration is not easy because it exposes our weaknesses.

The plan God implements for me will be different than the one he implements for you. Ask God for your plan and follow that plan. The plan may involve incarceration. I had to be incarcerated to prevent the granting of my death wish. I took a lot of risks. I never expected to live past the age of 21.

I failed to make good plans. I did not see a long life. I did not see myself living into my 40's. A long life was a fantasy and not an expectation. A man must always have a plan. I let the enemy highjack my mind. He told me I had no future.

Goodbye

Whenever I hear stories of redemption I notice several similarities. The first similarity is the exodus. Almost every man and woman I meet state how they left their familiar environment to mature. A man may need to leave his city or home to grow into a whole person. Transformation is almost impossible without leaving home. Our negative habits and lack of purpose are derived from our homes. The people we spent our lives with are the reason we became the way we are. It is hard to change when the people we are close to put us in a box. Once a man is labeled, it is extremely hard to change it.

It is impossible to fit into a box and continue to grow. Our parents label us when we are young. It may be necessary to separate from your parents. In some cases, your friends label you and refuse to allow you to change. A reputation can imprison you. Say Goodbye to old friends. Say goodbye to negative family members.

Another reason to leave home is because of the atmosphere. In order to move to a higher level in the world, you must surround yourself with people who have made it to the higher level. You cannot remain among people who have no desire to improve themselves. Poor people with poor mentalities enjoy poverty. Their vision causes them to believe that a state of poverty is where they belong. I had to get away from the negative peers I surrounded myself with during my teenage years. The poverty minded people envy the successful people. The envious men taught me to hate the wealthy.

I had to leave Virginia to become a whole man. I moved to Georgia in 1998. This change of residence allowed me to see what type of person I really was. I had the freedom to choose my own activities. I did not have to impress anyone or submit to the expectations of my clique. This opportunity to be free from my reputation allowed introspection.

I began to recognize how I was only engaging in certain behaviors because of my environment. I would not have done those things if I lived somewhere else. Fist fighting was one of the things I did because of my environment. I was not looking for fights, but they always happened. I did not fight in Atlanta, Georgia. I talked my way out of confrontations. Everyone does not want to be a fighter. I was surprised how many men were not interested in confrontations. Everyone is not interested in being a thug.

Forgiveness

Psalm 25:18 Look upon mine affliction and my pain; and forgive all my sins.

Forgiveness is another aspect of the plan God implements in a person's life. Forgiveness is when a man or woman gives someone who violated him or her a pardon. Forgiveness is a free gift awarded from one person to another. This free gift cannot be earned. In most cases, the person who is forgiven does not deserve to be forgiven.

Forgiveness is important because rebellion and hatred are symptoms of pain. Juvenile delinquents are corrupted after being hurt by someone. Some of the pain that is internalized comes from abuse. The abuse could have been physical, mental, sexual, or verbal. These issues plague many children and adults. I had to forgive people for the unjust treatment I received in the past. It was impossible to move forward in life holding on to a negative past.

The person who does not forgive will transfer that pain to another person. I read about men who are physically abused always physically abuse someone else. The cycle is continued. The first victim must forgive his attacker to prevent the cycle from continuing.

Neglect is an issue that causes pain that must be extinguished. Many juvenile delinquents feel a sense of neglect. A child without supervision is a child who will live in fear. A child without supervision is a child who lives with anger. A fearful and angry child will develop enemies. A neglected child will make his friends his enemies because he or she does not know who to trust. A child will look for opposition because he or she lacks guidance. Sometimes children rebel because they want someone to control them. The energy that is contained within children must be properly directed. Children are not supposed to live without leadership.

When a man or woman is preparing for restoration; he or she must forgive his or hers parents for neglect. I was locked up with men who had anger problems. The feelings of neglect caused them to believe that no one truly loved them. We must forgive religious leaders who lied and school teachers who insulted us. So much of our self-hatred was taught to us. People see the greatness within you and want to diminish it.

Job 5:2 For wrath kills a foolish man, And envy slays a simple one.

Jealousy and envy kill the owner of it. The people who are jealous and envious of you will seek to destroy you because they hate themselves. But you must forgive them. Jesus said forgive others the same way I forgave you.

Forgiveness is the topic I have heard taught thousands of times. Forgiveness is necessary because it allows you to give other people a new account. When you give people a new account, they will want to give you a new account. Do not be deceived. You hurt some people too. There are many people who had to forgive you during your lifetime. When you treat people as if they never mistreated you, they will want to learn how to treat you as if you never mistreated them.

Forgiveness is a great method of learning the true definition of love. Forgiveness is what Jesus gave us. We become like him when we do not hold on to the pain inflicted on us by other people. Love is the instigator of forgiveness.

Daniel 9:9 To the Lord our God belong mercies and forgiveness, though we have rebelled against him;

Love

The third element that I witnessed in my own transformation and the conversion of others is love. My definition of love shifted when I learned about God. The definition of love that I held was the wrong definition. When I began to learn about God, the correct definition was given to me. I immediately realized that I never loved anyone before.

Love is a free gift just like forgiveness. Love must be given to anyone and everyone you come into contact with. The same God created us all. We must understand what love is and then use it to improve our lives. With love we can improve our community. The true definition of love frees us to make the necessary changes in ourselves. The definition of love that we have been taught in the past was not love. It was manipulation. We only loved what we could control. We only loved the things that made us happy.

The definition of love that many of us learned was centered on personal gain. The definition of love that I accepted and exhibited was based on my comfort level. I loved what I could control. I loved what I could dictate. I loved the activities I naturally succeeded in. I loved the challenge that I received from sports and stubborn women. I did not understand that love only begins when my needs were removed from the equation.

True love does not involve any self-service. True love involves seeking the comfort and well-being of another person ahead of my own needs. True love is what Jesus did for people who did not love him. Jesus paid a debt that he did not earn. True love is honoring, respecting, and forgiving people who don't deserve it. True love is making a decision to place the needs of others ahead of your own need for comfort. True love is exhibited by extending mercy. Love is a decision.

Love is a decision that I had to practice. I had to practice love as an adult because I never knew what it was as a child. I had to learn how to love my wife. I had to learn how to love my children. Once I learned what love is, I had to apply it to people and situations. The application of love was accompanied by fear. When I chose to love others I became vulnerable. This vulnerability is the reason hard core men do not want to experience love.

I remember the way I treated women before and after I was incarcerated. I would not allow true emotions to enter the relationship. I knew that my trust and loyalty would be threatened. I was already in a state of brokenness. I did not want to be in a position that may cause me to feel worse.

The biggest challenge facing a hardened man is to love himself. Loving yourself is a challenge. We have been told by everyone in our lives that we lack character and self-control. We are constantly being told what is wrong with us. At school we are told what we need to successful and not taught how to use what is already inside us. At church we are told that we are sinful people who deserve hell. The television tells us that we are sex addicted fools. When the True and Living God tells us that we are supposed to love ourselves and become his disciples; it is hard to believe. When God tells you that all you need is him, it makes no sense. When I learned to listen to God, I no longer cared what other people said. I was finally able to love myself. Regardless of my past.

Emotions

When I was released from state custody in 1997, I thought I knew what I was looking for in a woman. I also thought I had a firm understanding of my emotions. I had no clue how lost I was. My distorted mind caused me to hurt women and myself. My distorted emotions led me to the wrong women. I was not thinking clearly.

When God begins to restore a man, he reorders and resets his emotions. The culture we live in causes some of these emotional disorders. I would become happy when I was expected to be sad. I would be sad when I was expected to be happy. When sadness becomes the norm, you will create a situation that keeps you sad.

The years of associating with the wrong people caused me to develop a disoriented conscience. Believe it or not, the people close to you may not want you to be happy. I had trouble trusting honest women and I enjoyed the drama that accompanied dishonest women. The stress seemed exciting.

Human emotions are intended to assist us in maintaining relationships. Our emotions are designed to inform us when we are making good decisions. Our emotions are also designed to impose feelings of guilt whenever you make a bad decision. When a man's emotional state becomes unstable, he adopts the same mentality he implemented as a child. That man may become childish, immature, and selfish. At his worst, the unstable man will become violent and destructive.

Emotions must be in order to survive in the community after a lengthy confinement in jail or prison. I had several moments when I lost my temper after my release. I was not prepared to handle the responsibilities of independent living. Life is unpredictable and imbalanced. The people that I depended on were the same ones who mistreated and abandoned me. The people that I trusted were the ones who betrayed me. The world is full of users and abusers. The people who don't know God will misuse and abuse you. That is all they know. I had to accept that fact.

I wanted to believe that problems and issues disappeared in one night. The truth is that men avoid their problems by getting high. We also avoid our problems by finding pleasant distractions. I could not handle the everyday stress of living in this world. I had a habit of disconnecting from my responsibilities. I would also isolate myself to avoid conflicts. My emotional state was very volatile. When I realized I could not hide from life's challenges and obstacles, I started to heavily medicate myself. The weed and the alcohol is the prescription offered by the community. Doctors offer prescription medicine to alleviate anxiety. Both substances are dangerous. Neither of them are needed. We must know our Creator.

Whole and Broken

The broken man just wants to obtain comfort. When you are broken, you will accept the nearest source of comfort that is available. The first person or the first source that claims to be able to ease the pain is accepted by men who need relief. The relief comes in different forms. The different forms of relief are: religious activity, gang affiliations, music, sports, sex, drugs, alcohol, and work. These are a few of the options that relieve pain.

These options become pleasant distractions from the root of the discomfort. The internal conflicts still exist. But we can ignore the conflicts as long as our relief systems function. In my opinion, the biggest challenge facing a broken man or a broken woman is admitting that he or she is broken. We have the technology and the resources to hide our faults and fears. A broken man can hide his fragile heart by buying a new car or a big new house. A man in a state of depression can hide his illness and fear while in a dark, smoke-filled nightclub. A broken man can mask his weakened condition with a college degree. Broken women change their hair color to feel brand new. Pleasant distractions provide temporary relief.

There is a reason men and women sleep with new partners every week. The broken people are searching for a new high. The sex is just a method of experiencing a new high. The new partner is also not aware of the faults in his or hers partner. Men and women want new sex partners because the old partner knows that he or she is not perfect. We hide our faults. The new high is pretending to be flawless for a night.

Admitting that you need help is very disturbing. We are taught at an early age not to expect more than we deserve. At an early age, we are told our worth and value to the world. Early in a boy or girls life, he or she is given a rating that becomes a subconscious measure of success. That rating is implanted into a child's mind passively. Once the idea is implanted, that child is left on autopilot. A child in autopilot will respond to certain stimuli instinctively for many years. He or she may never reach higher than he or she has been taught to reach.

I wrote about the stress involved in being released from prison. I wrote about the dangers of being disconnected from God. It is very easy to focus on the problems and the dangers that destroy the lives of men and women. Anyone can complain about the conflicts, injustice, and pain life consists of, but how many people have the solution to the pain and the injustice? This writing is in vain if I cannot provide a solid answer to the problem.

The situations we get into are positive and negative lessons. All of the lessons are designed to make us whole again. The bad days in our lives are lessons. Some lessons are more painful than others. The lessons all lead back to our God. The pain and the stress force us to find the resolution to our lives. Or quit. Please do not quit.

Our Creator wants us to become whole men. I am in the process of becoming a whole man. A whole man is a holy man. It is our troubles that force us to desire the mind and presence of God. A person once said "You will get sick and tired of being sick and tired. Then you will seek God and give up trying to control your own life."

A whole man will want to know his Creator. God will take a broken man and make him whole again. The Bible said only the holy ones will enter the Kingdom of Heaven. We become unholy while living here on this Earth. We lose our focus and attempt to live without God's guidance. This happens to everyone. Eventually, the path we lead causes trouble and distress. Sin breaks our spirit and ruins our relationships. That broken spirit must be mended. Only the original Creator can take a broken man and form him into a whole man again.

If all men are broken and unholy, it is not wise to listen to another man in search of advice and repair. Only the Creator can offer true guidance and healing. How can another help if he too is in need of restoration. Broken people cannot help broken people. Two broken people working together will only find more complicated methods to remain shattered. Jesus Christ is the whole God-Man who makes us whole. Learn of him and be repaired. It is the only way that worked for me.

Autopilot

The autopilot state can be positive or negative. The child in autopilot will automatically self-destruct or overachieve for the remainder of his or hers life. Autopilot may also lead a boy or girl to remain the same for his or hers entire life. The autopilot state is when an idea is embedded into a child's mind and he or she follows that idea subconsciously without any more input. I was an example of a person on an autopilot program. I was programed to deny my gifts and except the world's definition of me. I had to oppose God to refuse my gift.

An autopilot program can be positive or negative. A positive example of autopilot is the privileged child who is born wealthy. That child will always work hard to avoid poverty because he or she expects to win and succeed. The children of wealthy successful parents are taught at an early age to succeed. The children who only accept victory never settle for second place. The wealthy child is programmed to study and exhibit proper manners in public. He or she protects his or hers image. The wealthy child learns critical thinking skills so he or she can preserve the family fortune after his or hers parents are dead.

The negative program keeps men and women operating beneath their preordained levels. People living as underachievers become comfortable on that level. They are taught to accept that low level. Men and women who accept defeat will reject anyone who attempts to improve their lives. People who do not expect to live better will resist asking for help. Most underachievers avoid opportunities for self-improvement. An underachiever cannot admit that he or she needs help because it will reveal that he or she can do better.

The autopilot program affects men and women in various ways. Religious traditions are based on the autopilot program. Children are indoctrinated with lies by their parents and never question them. A person in autopilot will not question the information that is imparted to him or her. The autopilot system destroys critical thinking in its victim.

The True and Living God expects us to be critical thinkers. The Bible contains many scriptures that show us how often God told his children to test him to prove he is real. God does not want us to hope in nothing. He provides proof that he is involved in his children's lives.

How many people want to do better? How many people expect to do better? How many people are willing to give up their friends and families to become better? How many people are willing to give up what they are to become someone better? In autopilot, a man may not know that it is possible to live better than his current status. What program are you following?

Learn critical thinking. Erase the autopilot program. Question what you know and what you believe. The people who do not want to be questioned are the ones who want to control your mind.

The teachers God provides to his children are genuine and transparent. We enjoy the questions because they give us an opportunity to learn more about our God. We have no interest in mind control. We want to be questioned because everyone learns more. There is no shame in Jesus Christ. It is all about him.

Images

The pain and the stain that remains from living the illegal life becomes a badge of honor to the misguided. Our culture is immersed in various forms of idolatry. Our culture is not a God-centered culture. Children are steered towards the wrong types of leadership. Children are guided to submit to people who have the wrong image of success. The current religious systems and the social commentators worship men and women who have sinful backgrounds. The children need to be exposed to leadership that had enough wisdom to avoid prison. The children should be taught to respect athletes who do not have tattoos and thug images.

The men and women who never broke the law should be exalted more than the people who have been in trouble. Street credibility should be a negative brand. Tim Duncan is a NBA champion. He does not have a signature basketball shoe. NBA players who are convicted felons have signature basketball shoes. Tim Duncan does not have a criminal record and he never receives negative press. Why is Tim Duncan not the most popular NBA player?

The present concept of street credibility derived from the hip-hop culture. The men and women who subscribe to the religion of hip-hop want street credibility. The children are taught to respect adults and authority figures with street credibility. This idea that street credibility is noble must be eradicated. Too many teenagers intentionally commit crimes and acts of degradation just to get a reputation. The stain of a criminal record is no longer a negative mark. A criminal record is not a blemish in a person's life anymore. The negative past is now viewed as a medal of honor. The main issue with the worship of people with negative pasts is that the children begin to expect failure. The children lose the fear of shame and infamy. Teenagers think that they must learn from their mistakes. This is wrong thinking. The wise men learn from other peoples mistakes.

Street credibility is something that alters the image of a man. A man is supposed to be a person with integrity. Infamy is viewed as good but it should be viewed as a stain. The wisest men I have met were not formal criminals. They did not have street credibility. They avoided making mistakes because their honor and integrity were more important than earning respect from people in the neighborhood. When a teenager is taught the true definition of manhood, he will avoid becoming a person who believes it is okay to have a rebellious past.

The first time I was locked, in 1995, up I thought it was acceptable. I was not upset at all. I was comfortable in the juvenile prison. I had friends who were already confined in the detention center. Being in the juvenile prison was just a stop along the path to building a hooligan reputation. I was more afraid to get out because I knew I would come back.

Jail does not provoke fear in most teenagers. Jail is just a school of hard knocks. No different than high school. Jail is viewed as an alternative school. Some feel more comfortable in a jail than a Bible study. The jail is no longer a place of punishment. Jail is now an escape from reality. The image of an institution affects the people who are viewing it from the outside. Teenagers do not fear prison until they get there. It is too late then.

These are all symptoms of not fearing God. A person with no fear of God will do anything he or she desires. The person with no fear of God only sees the wrong images because he or she is walking in darkness.

Acceptance

How do we accept God and his law? When does a man submit to his plan? Is it possible to submit to something that you don't know? I did not submit to God until my whole life was almost ruined. Why does a man have to lose it all before he chooses to obey God? The path to ultimate victory is the path we voluntarily forfeit. Why?

I rejected God and his ideas at the beginning of my transformation. I did not understand my purpose during this period of my life. I would hear clear messages in my spirit. I thought it was God communicating with me but I was not mature enough to respond. In some instances, I did not want to respond. God would give an instruction that I did not want to obey. Jesus Christ places a demand on his sons. No other God can do that. There is no other True God.

I adapted to my self-medicated, prideful life. I thought that I was playing my pre-determined role in the world. The movies show so many black sheep and failures that I thought I was just playing my role in the world. I could not accept the fact that God wanted something more. I really did not know him. My mind needed to be renewed.

Everything I learned in the past was wrong. The revelation that I was full of the wrong knowledge sparked fear in my heart. The drugs that I used were helping me cope with a seared conscience. The alcohol allowed me to ease my pain from past experiences. I used my selfish pride as motivation to continue living. The pride I possessed gave me the strength to work every day and get educated, but that same pride did not allow me to adjust my course. I was determined to survive my own way. I wanted to use God's power without Him.

The traits that make a man strong and valuable are also the same traits that lead to his demise. The strength a person puts into developing a life is the same energy he or she uses to maintain that life. As a result, that high level of energy is recruited to keep God out of a man's life. The

35,000 different religions on Earth are the proof that men want the power of God but do not want the True God involved in our affairs.

Future/Past

One of the major lessons I learned since the start of my conversion is that I lived in the past instead of the future. One of the biggest mistakes I made was not preparing for the future. I allowed myself to remain in the past. By focusing on the past, I would maintain my old way of thinking. The old thinking would cause me to repeat and relive my past. I had a habit of making the same old mistakes with new people.

The child who is demoralized in high school will produce a situation that will demoralize him again. The child who is publicly shamed in high school will be find people to publicly shame him again. The old way of thinking must be discarded. The problems, pain, and trauma from the past must be left in the past.

The future has not been determined. But the way we form our thinking and identity propels us to repeat our pasts. The teenagers who were creative and successful early in life become creative and successful in the future. The teenagers who were failures and weak in the past turn out to be failures and weak in the future. Our pasts become our future because we rely on information from the past to determine our future. People fail to make the necessary changes in the present that will make the future different from the past.

The future will be determined by the decisions we make today. The future should not be determined by the mistakes and shortcomings from the past. Many people only use their negative past to formulate ideas for the future. People need to adopt new ideas to begin a new and better future. In order to transform your life, you need to transform the way you think.

Outside the Gate

I wrote these ideas to assist anyone who is living outside the gate. The person who is living outside the gate must enter God's shelter to survive. I was released from a physical prison and continued to self-destruct. My mind was imprisoned with a lie. Many other lies were exposed after my 21st birthday.

God exposed the things that were damaging my state of mind. My mind was full of misunderstandings and wrong ideas about life. God completely revealed my past to me. I could not be made whole if I continued to ignore my past.

The troubles I endured before I was incarcerated the first time, continued to exist after I was released. The changes that I needed to improve my life could not be performed by a long stay in a prison. The issues that I needed to address required a God who knew my deepest thoughts. Only God knew my deepest fears. I was not aware of what was inside me. The corruption inside me existed for so long it became normal. The transformation that I needed could only be performed by the original designer.

Incarceration may be the method the Creator used to save my life. The Creator had a plan for my life before I arrived. I did not know what to do with my life. No one could tell me what to do with my life. Most people do not know how to manage their own lives. It was not wise to expect them to assist me. Only God knows how I am supposed to function in his world. Prison was just an educational setback on the road to perfection. I was incarcerated four times. Two of them were just warnings. I was released after a brief lesson.

A man or woman is not free just because he or she is not in a prison cell. The ultimate freedom is living within God's gate. The ultimate freedom is living without shame and guilt. The ultimate freedom is obeying God and allowing him to handle your responsibilities. God's gate is the rules and boundaries that he set to preserve our souls. It is a gate. Every man and woman can enter and exit at any time.

The gate God established for our lives is designed to protect us from destruction. The gate God established is designed to promote a peaceful existence with other people. God's gate is also designed to keep enemies out. He guards the gate. The gate prevents communities from dividing.

The purpose of the Word of God that I now understand is that it is designed for an imperfect world. God provided his word because he knew we would go astray. I didn't know that he was providing a history of the world and simple ideas on how to live a sin free life. I did not know God personally. I knew he was real but I did not know how to relate to him. Most of us do not know God. We want to know God, but our culture separates us from him. The people who claim to know Jesus do a great job of misrepresenting him.

Attempting to live outside of God's gate is living in dysfunction. A dysfunctional life is a life that will end up in a physical prison. Dysfunctional people live lives of sin and quiet desperation. The sin creates a distance between man and God. The quiet desperation leads people to attach themselves to groups that they should avoid. I can't help but regret accepting the lie that I would not live to see my 21st birthday. I know I would have made different choices if I was going to live past the age of 21.

While you are in the physical prison, the dominant thought is I wish I was free. Just ask yourself what you want to be free from. Do you want to be free from all authority figures? That is impossible. Do you want to be free from God's authority? That is also impossible. What do you want to be free of? How do you define free?

We must know God. We are already religious.

We must know God. We are born religious.

Living outside the prison means nothing without purpose and God's vision. Freedom also involves removing the lies that imprison your thoughts. God will remove the lies you live with. The lies are an invisible prison that will destroy your life. Only God can restore our minds to a pure state. That pure state of mind is a taste of heaven.

The Gospel

Jesus loves you and there is nothing you can do to stop him. He knew you were not perfect before you committed your first sin. He knew you would attempt to control your own life before you knew you would fail. Jesus is the one who paid your sin debt before you were born. The gospel is good news because your guilt and shame is removed by the one who will eventually judge you. The judge is the savior, you cannot lose.

Jesus showed us the way to live. The concepts that Jesus Christ taught contradict most of what we learn from other people. Jesus taught us to use our minds more than our muscle. Jesus taught us that the way to wealth is not fast and illegal. Jesus taught us that we worry and lose peace because we attempt to do his job. We need to allow the Creator to continue creating. Our lives will manifest more peace, harmony, and love. Jesus said, "seek the kingdom of God first, and all of its righteousness. Then we will have everything we need."

Jesus is the Creator. He can rightfully judge you because he is the one who created you. He knows exactly what you were born to accomplish. He knows how much potential you possess. He knows your weaknesses because he knows who influenced your mind. The gospel is good news because you can reestablish the perfect relationship you had with your Creator before sin separated you.

Jesus is salvation because no one else paid our sin debt. I studied many religions and many cultures. Only one person claimed to pay for my sins. Only one person claimed to be the sinless Son of God. Only one person loved his enemies as much as he loved his friends. Jesus is salvation. No one else claimed to pay our sin debt.

Sin is the one item that I could never eradicate. Sin is the one item that I could not remove from my life. I remember attempting to find perfect people so I could live sin free. This fantasy never lasted long. The perfect people I found would eventually disappoint me. I studied many other religions because I wanted to find a way to eliminate sin and injustice. I wanted to perfect the world before I knew Jesus. I wanted my first son to live in a world without pain. I thought I could find a way to make that happen. Everywhere I looked for answers described Jesus Christ. The path of the truth seeker will lead to Jesus Christ.

I was very adamant about my son not being incarcerated. I did not want him to smoke and drink. I had this idea that I could protect him from suffering. The more I wanted to change the world, the worse my behavior became. It began to feel like God himself was telling me that the world was not getting worse. He was telling me that I was getting worse.

This consciousness became crystal clear when Jesus revealed himself to me. The problem was not my motives. The problem was believing I could change the world apart from God. Jesus works through his servants. We cannot transform the world ourselves. Jesus Christ will not transform the world. He will restore one man at a time.

The ultimate goal is not avoiding the physical prison to feel free. The ultimate goal is to live inside the gate God established to protect us from our own evil. Living inside his gate is not bondage. Living inside God's gate and following his rules is true freedom. The gate keeps negativity out, while containing positivity within. When we live in God's kingdom we will not have to worry about breaking man's laws. The physical prison is no longer an issue.

This writing is intended to inform any young adult or teenager who is incarcerated, physically or spiritually, that existing outside the gate is not peaceful or healthy. When I was released from the juvenile prison in 1997 I was nervous. My soul knew something was out of order. I had no goals, vision, purpose, or plan. I did not live according to my intended design because I did not know the designer. My soul never rested. I was hungry for something that would bring me peace of mind. I knew a God existed but I hated religion.

I am now 34 years old. The last seven years of my life taught me that being in communion with God is the true freedom. Living in communion with God gave my soul rest because every moment of my life has meaning. The good days are lessons. The bad days are lessons. The eradication of sin removed my fear of the police and potential enemies. Living in sin created a fear and resentment of the police and other authority figures. My sinful lifestyle also created conflict with other men. Most importantly, I had internal conflicts that needed to be resolved. Living out of fellowship with God, led to my physical incarceration. Living in fellowship with God led to my physical and mental freedom.

THE END

2015: THE COST OF FREEDOM

I am now prepared to publish this book. I have been free from SIN for over eight years. The freedom is a new experience. The freedom has produced a condition of anxiety and joy. I feel the anxiety and joy at the same time. The anxiety is felt because I do not know what to do with my freedom. The joy is felt because I no longer fear the wrath of God. Anxiety is very similar to fear. The question now becomes; why feel fear?

Every man, woman, and child knows the bondage associated with SIN. Humans are always addicted to something. Humans are always negative about something. Humans are always controlled by their animal instincts. That bondage becomes normal and a person accepts his or hers disposition. That bondage produced a man in me that became the new normal. I already explained how we trade slavery for liberty. I was secure in that animal, obsessive-compulsive, alcoholic, skirt-chasing man. I was comfortable allowing myself to be angry and impulsive. If felt normal. I knew what to expect. Now I am changed. God called it free.

I mention these aspects of character and lifestyle because I changed and realized I did not know what to expect anymore. When I changed; my attitude changed. When I changed; my worldview shifted. The changes in my life removed old friends and invited new friends. I felt the anxiety associated with freedom because I began to realize I was no longer in control of my life. The True and Living God was now in control. I was not bound to my old animal behaviors anymore.

A good example of God's freedom is a man on the moon. He has nothing holding him while he is walking. The lack of gravity allows him to bounce in any direction. But nothing in him can hold him to the surface. The man must be attached to a structure or object to remain steady. When SIN lost its power over my life; I had to find a new structure to attach myself to for a steady life. My soul was alive again. It became a new life. The joy was present but I had nothing to hold on. My old life was gone. Starting over will prevent a person from giving his or hers life to God.

Another example of the true freedom Jesus provides is when a car is idling next to a stationary object. The car may be in a parking lot. Am I moving, or is the car next to me moving?

How do you know if you moving? There are two methods to determine if you are moving. The scenery will change if you moving. If you sitting in an idle car, the scenery will not change. The view from the windshield will not alter. The same people and places and buildings will remain in front of you. You will know you not moving because the same view is in front of you.

This is our lives. If you not moving; you will see the same thing each day. If your life is not going anywhere; you will not change your worldview. You will see the same pain, obstacles, people, and negativity. Jesus keeps us moving.

Our worldview is always changing. He removes the old pain, obstacles, people, and negativity.

The other method that proves whether or not a person is moving is to look at a stationary object. If the distance is changing between you and the stationary object; it is you who is moving. A stationary object cannot move. If the distance is shorter, you are moving closer to the object. If the distance is greater, you are moving further from the object. This concept applies to our lives.

What stationary object are you using to determine your travel? What stationary object are you moving closer to; or further away from? I needed to measure my new life. I could not be satisfied with the new emotion. How do I know if I was becoming good and righteous? How do I know if I am becoming delusional? What am I measuring my development against? The only assessment tool for the soul is the Bible. I read the Bible nonstop for years. This is how I measured my growth.

Every man needs to hold onto something. My issue is when God obtained control of my life; HE was holding me. I had to learn that I was no longer doing what I wanted to do. It became easy to live with that passion and untamed energy. I could measure myself against other men. The True and Living God wants his son's to measure themselves according to the Bible. HE wants his son's to become like Jesus. I could no longer be satisfied with my performance. I could no longer be satisfied with a mediocre existence. There is a cost to this eternal freedom.

I was born again in 2006. I have learned many lessons since 2006. I have witnessed spiritual conversions in other men. I have witnessed other men avoid a spiritual conversion. The light provokes fear. The momentum God immerses a man into produces a panic. The panic is caused because of a change in worldview. The newness is disorienting. I understand why men ignore the call from heaven. God will completely transform a man. That man will not recognize himself after the transformation. The only way a man can avoid the call is to turn his back against the light. He dooms himself.

In order to avoid the light, a man must turn his back on God. If Jesus is standing in front of you, he is standing on the path of righteousness. When a man says no, he can only travel in the opposite direction. That direction is the path to total destruction.

It is amazing that a man will choose destruction over redemption. I did it so many times. I chose to be destroyed over and over again. Why? Now I see other men do it. I see young, teenage inmates who choose to be destroyed by SIN; instead of surrendering to the will of God. I have adult friends who choose to control their own lives. The first thing we must realize is that we all did the best we can do with our lives. Just look at the results. How can anyone state, "I don't need God!"

The Bible has many examples of men and women who chose to ignore the Creator. These men and women were eventually destroyed because of their own decisions. King Saul committed suicide after rebelling against God. Samson lost his eyes and killed himself; after rebelling against God. King Solomon lost ten tribes from the kingdom of Israel after rebelling against God. Abraham disobeyed God and produced an illegitimate heir. Ishmael has been a conflict in this world ever since that incident. These people were examples for us today. Ironically, today we seem to make the same mistakes these people made 4000 years ago.

Freedom is not free. The cost of freedom is obedience. Obedience is revealed in progress. Obedience is witnessed by the amount of transformation a person exhibits. I knew I was changing when others told me I changed. All I know is that I was feeling so ashamed of my past that I followed the Bible to see if I could find peace. I didn't have anything else. I didn't want anything else. Obeying God is easy when a man does not want anything else. Maybe that was why God allowed me to live like a pagan for so long. Maybe he wanted me to be full of my animal cravings before he changed me. This would ensure I would not turn back.

I meet other men who were transformed early in life. I had chances to be saved as a teen but it never happened. I could not see the benefit in being religious. It did not help the older people who claimed to be saved. I did not want to be like them. The way God changed me was perfect. I was at home praying. Just me and my wife. I heard the call and knew it was my Creator.

In retrospect, I see how HE was in my life the entire time. Life is all about knowing God. Our good choices and our bad choices only prove the Word of God to be true. Life is not about sports, entertainment, food, money, fame, education, power, sex, or religion. It is about knowing HIM. John chapter 17 states that, "eternal life is to know God, the

One True God." Life is about knowing HIM. The journey is designed to lead us to HIM.

RESULTS

The results of the transformation are all positive. The new freedom scared me. I had no method of seeing what the Creator was guiding me towards. I did not know what I could accomplish with the remainder of my life. I originally never viewed my future past the age of 21. I was 28 years old when I was born again. Now what?

I was compelled to enroll in college by my Hebrew teacher. He told me I would need to increase my level of education. He also stated that I would get older with or without an education. Why not get one? Use my spare time on self-improvement. He also stated that enrolling in college will surround me with better people. Colleges and universities attract people who are doers and not dreamers. I earned a Bachelor's Degree in criminal justice. I will have my Master's Degree, in psychology, in the summer of 2015.

I never considered studying criminal justice and psychology. I see how the Creator is guiding my life by analyzing the results. My past is in accord with my present. Everything I studied and endured in the past is related to what I am currently engaged in. Helping others overcome their situations and recognize their need to obey their Creator. Studying criminal justice and psychology is also helping me understand my past and why I made the decisions that I made. Teenagers are desperate for guidance and attention.

Another accomplishment that proved God is God involves my family. I have been married over 11 years. How many young couples survive 10 years of marriage in the new millennium? The statistics are very low. My wife and I met 16 years ago. The Creator knew who he wanted me to marry. He also gave us three healthy children to nurture. It was all about HIM. It is all about establishing HIS will on Earth. Our family reflects his creative glory. We show others that he is

God. The fact that we survived the many obstacles that manifested in our lives is proof that obeying the Bible is the way to freedom. Freedom is living in HIS will.

The result of my conversion is evident in my family. My three children are living in communion with God. My children tell their friends and school teachers about God. We live in his presence. This is how we are supposed to exist. The outside influences are just entertainment and distractions. The hip-hop culture does not promote communion with God. The way to nurture a child is to guide him or her with God's word. The cost of my freedom is a responsibility to teach my children.

Freedom is not free. Just like love is not free. Freedom is only true if it does not break a law. Freedom is bound by rules and obligations. Love is also bound by an obligation. Love is only love if it attached to something. You cannot love nothing. Love is attached to my wife. I cannot hurt my wife. I have an obligation to my wife. I love my children. That love compels me to go to work and provide for them. God's way is true freedom, but it has boundaries.

Walking with God is a journey that is exciting. Not knowing the future is humbling and peaceful. I did not like it in the past. I always thought I could control the future with my will and hard work. God proves that man has no true power. What we consider power is actually pride and rebellion.

The life of obedience is not an easy life. My wife and I are tempted to follow the pattern of the world every day. We endured many days and nights with no food or money. We endured the feelings of animosity and hate from other Christian families. We endured loneliness and depression many weeks. These incidents only showed us the truth of the Bible. These incidents proved to us that God is the only one who can guide or lives. The struggle and the stress revealed our weaknesses and insecurities. The lack of resources showed us who are God sent friends were. The uncomfortable moments in life are designed to make us perfect. Following God is just as hard as living without God. The difference is purpose.

Following God leads to perfection and his will. He does not destroy his children. He sends work to make them pure and strong. Disobeying God leads to God himself destroying you for becoming his enemy. What is your purpose?

I know my purpose now. HE showed me. My life makes sense now. My family is whole. I forgave the people I needed to forgive. I learned to forgive myself. The Bible taught me the meaning of love and grace. Jesus is the king, and he always was the king.

Whoever is reading this, you must know, there is no other way. Love, hate, justice, and forgiveness only met at one place in human history. These four elements are essential for our lives to function properly. We experience these four elements each day. These four elements met at the cross on Mount Calvary. Jesus addressed every detail of our lives. In order to experience redemption, healing, and restoration; you need to know Jesus Christ.

If you do not want redemption, healing, or restoration; what is it that you want?

I am now 36 years old with a wife and three children. I recall the life I was living in high school and my early 20's. The decisions I was making were based on deceit and anger. I would make decisions based on someone else's expectations. I felt deceived because I could not trust the people who were close to me. I felt angry because I could not remove them from my life. I now realize that many of these people were suffering from the same anxieties and fears. The whole world appears out of order. We live in a world that is in rebellion to its Creator. We all need restoration. When I learned these truths, I was able to forgive others and not be bitter anymore. I hope you can be born again, too. Walk in truth and light.

<u>John 3:3</u> *Jesus answered and said unto him, Verily, verily, I say unto thee, Except a man be born again, he cannot see the kingdom of God.*

<u>John 3:21</u> *But he who does the truth comes to the light, that his deeds may be clearly seen, that they have been done in God."*

2 Corinthians 4:6

For it is the God who commanded light to shine out of darkness, who has shone in our hearts to give the light of the knowledge of the glory of God in the face of Jesus Christ.